SPECIAL ZEALAND'S SOUTH ISLAND TRAVEL GUIDE 2024

Exploring the Natural Wonders of New Zealand

Nameem Rumberg

TABLE OF CONTENTS

Legal and Practical Considerations

CHAPTER SEVEN

Conclusion

INTRODUCTION

Welcome to the charming domain of Aotearoa, where rich scenes, remarkable mountains, and clear lakes combine to make the captivating material of New Zealand's South Island. As you leave on an excursion through this safe house of normal magnificence, social wealth, and experience, our fastidiously organized travel guide, "Finding Heaven: A Thorough Manual for Special New Zealand's South Island in the year 2024," coaxes you to investigate the marvels that anticipate.

In 2024, we welcome you to navigate the uncommon embroidery of New Zealand's South Island, an objective prestigious for its exceptional mix of Maori legacy, unrivaled view, and outside exercises that will light your soul of experience. This movement guide isn't simply a summary of spots to visit; it is a vital aspect for opening the mysteries of a locale that flawlessly winds around together practice, innovation, and regular quality.

As you flip through the pages of this aide, you will find an abundance of data intended to change your excursion into an extraordinary odyssey. From the snow-covered pinnacles of the Southern Alps to the perfect sea shores of the West Coast, and from the energetic urban communities like Christchurch and Dunedin to the quiet fjords of Milford Sound, each side of the South Island unfurls a story ready to be found.

Our aide enlightens the notable milestones and digs into the unlikely treasures that lie outside of what might be expected. Drench yourself in the Maori culture, enjoy the kinds of nearby food, and embrace the glow of Kiwi friendliness. Whether you are a courageous pioneer looking for adrenaline-siphoning undertakings or a peacefulness searcher longing for tranquil scenes, the South Island brings something to the table for each insightful voyager.

Moreover, this version isn't simply a depiction of the present; it's a window into the eventual fate of movement. With refreshed data on manageable practices, eco-accommodating facilities, and the capability the travel industry drives, we urge you to investigate New Zealand with a pledge to protect the regular ponders that make this island heaven genuinely unique.

Thus, leave on an excursion of disclosure, whether you are a first-time guest or a carefully prepared voyager getting back to savor the enchantment again. "Finding Heaven" is more than an aide; it's your friend in unwinding the mysteries of Special New Zealand's South Island in 2024. Allow the experience to start!

CHAPTER ONE

Land of the Long White Cloud

New Zealand at a Glance

In 2024, New Zealand's South Island stays a charming objective, dazzling explorers with its different scenes, rich social legacy, and a guarantee to maintainability. This island heaven, frequently alluded to as "Aotearoa" by the native Maori individuals, allures globe-trotters and nature lovers the same. We should dig into the novel features of New Zealand's South Island, offering a brief look into its magnificence, culture, and encounters that characterize this enthralling district.

Geographic Wonders:

Southern Alps:

The foundation of the South Island, the Southern Alps, is a lofty mountain range that cuts across the island, offering spectacular vistas. Aoraki/Mount Cook, the most elevated top, remains as a sentinel over this high wonderland, welcoming climbers, climbers, and nature sweethearts to investigate its snow-covered tops and perfect cold scenes.

Fiordland Public Park:

An UNESCO World Legacy Site, Fiordland Public Park is a demonstration of nature's glory. Transcending coves, flowing cascades, and thick rainforests make a sensational and perfect scenery. Milford Sound and Dicey Sound stand apart as notable objections, bringing guests into the core of this immaculate wild.

Social Embroidery:

Maori Impact:

The South Island gives proper respect to its native Maori legacy, clear in the inviting hongi (nose press) and the strong haka dance. Maori customs are saved in the mind boggling carvings of marae, the otherworldly gathering grounds, and the craft of narrating, furnishing guests with a rich social encounter.

European Legacy:

European impact is clear in beguiling urban communities like Christchurch and Dunedin, where Victorian engineering and noteworthy milestones tell the story of provincial pioneers. Historical centers and exhibitions feature the combination of Maori and European societies, making an agreeable mix exceptional to New Zealand.

Experience Heaven:

Queenstown:

Known as the experience capital of the world, Queenstown keeps on dazzling daredevils with its variety of exercises. Bungee hopping, skydiving, and fly sailing against the scenery of Lake Wakatipu and the Remarkables Mountains make an adrenaline-filled jungle gym.

Slogging and Climbing:

The South Island brags a broad organization climbing trails, drawing in nature devotees and explorers from around the globe. From the notable Milford Track to the far off Kepler Track, the different scenes give a range of journeying encounters, exhibiting the island's normal magnificence.

Biodiversity and Natural life:

Kaikoura:

Kaikoura, a waterfront town, offers an extraordinary mix of marine and earthbound untamed life encounters. Whale-watching outings divulge the finesse of monster sperm whales, while experiences with perky dolphins and seals give a cozy association the sea's occupants.

Interesting Birdlife:

The South Island is a safe house for birdwatchers, with endemic species like the Kea (high parrot) and Takahe adding to the island's biodiversity. Otago Promontory, specifically, is a birdwatcher's heaven with its different seabird settlements.

Manageability and Eco-The travel industry:
In 2024, New Zealand keeps on focusing on supportable the travel industry rehearses. Eco-accommodating facilities, protection drives, and local area commitment projects highlight the country's obligation to safeguarding the perfect excellence of the South Island for people in the future.

Maori Legacy and Social Knowledge

Saturated with antiquated customs and profoundly associated with the land, the Maori nation of New Zealand's South Island keep on imparting their rich legacy to guests in 2024. This energetic culture, woven into the texture of Aotearoa, unfurls through customary services, multifaceted carvings, and the warm accommodation of the Maori public. As we dig into the

Maori legacy of the South Island, we should investigate the social bits of knowledge and vivid encounters anticipating the individuals who look for a more profound comprehension of this native heritage.

Conventional Marae:

Wharenui and Wharekai:

A visit to a conventional Maori marae gives a brief look into the core of Maori culture. The wharenui (meeting house) embellished with unpredictable carvings and lively fine art fills in as a profound place for the local area. The wharekai (eating lobby) grandstands the meaning of common social occasions and shared feasts in Maori customs, cultivating a feeling of solidarity and association.

Powhiri Invite Function:

The powhiri, or welcome function, is a respected custom that denotes the start of a visit to a marae. Visitors are welcomed with the frightful hints of the karanga (call of welcome) and the cadenced haka, making way for a social trade that rises above language.

Haka: A Strong Articulation:

Social Exhibitions:

The haka, a stately dance known for its strong and musical developments, stays a focal part of Maori social exhibitions. In 2024, guests can observer haka exhibitions at far-reaching developments, celebrations, and, surprisingly, in ordinary settings, as the dance fills in as a unique articulation of character, strength, and solidarity.

Contemporary Variations:

While well established in custom, the haka has advanced to consolidate contemporary subjects. Exhibitions might reflect accounts of strength, social pride, and social issues, displaying the unique idea of Maori culture in the advanced time.

Inking and Carvings:

Ta Moko:

The craft of ta moko, or customary Maori inking, is a consecrated practice that conveys an individual's genealogy, personality, and life venture. In 2024, guests can investigate the meaning of ta moko through directed encounters, finding out about the social implications behind the many-sided plans that enhance the countenances and assemblages of the Maori public.

Whakairo (Cutting):

Carvings assume a critical part in Maori workmanship and narrating. From the complicated enumerating of wharenui to the more modest, versatile taonga (treasures), the whakairo mirrors the association between the Maori public and their current circumstance. Directed visits and studios offer experiences into the imagery and craftsmanship of these complicated carvings.

Social Celebrations:

Te Matatini:

Te Matatini, the public kapa haka (Maori performing expressions) celebration, assembles the most talented and enthusiastic entertainers from across New Zealand. In 2024, this biennial occasion features the variety of Maori performing expressions, including customary melodies, poi moves, and, obviously, the strong haka.

Neighborhood Festivities:

Past public occasions, neighborhood celebrations and festivities give valuable chances to observe and partake in Maori social practices. From music and dance to conventional cooking, these merriments offer a real and vivid experience.

Social Safeguarding and Schooling:

Social Focuses:

In 2024, social focuses devoted to Maori legacy keep on flourishing across the South Island. Foundations, for example, the Te Father Tongarewa Gallery in Wellington and the Canterbury Historical center in Christchurch highlight displays that teach guests about the set of experiences, workmanship, and customs of the Maori public.

Local area Drives:

Local area drove drives center around saving and rejuvenating the Maori language (Te Reo Maori), guaranteeing that people in the future acquire the extravagance of their social heritage. Language inundation programs, narrating meetings, and instructive effort add to the continuous conservation of Maori legacy.

Kiwi Way of Life

In 2024, the Kiwi lifestyle in New Zealand's South Island keeps on mirroring a one of a kind mix of laid-back enchant, outside excitement, and social extravagance. Prestigious for its accommodating local people, stunning scenes, and a guarantee to practical living, the South Island welcomes guests to drench themselves in the Kiwi lifestyle. We should dig into the particular features that shape this way of life, offering a brief look into the glow and validness that characterize the Kiwi experience.

Warm Neighborliness:

Nearby Amicability:

One of the central qualities of the Kiwi lifestyle is the warm and inviting nature of local people. In 2024, guests toward the South Island can anticipate authentic neighborliness, with local people frequently making a special effort to share stories, offer help, and give experiences into their lifestyle.

Local area Bonds:

The Kiwi people group soul is fit as a fiddle in towns and urban communities across the South Island. Local area occasions, ranchers' business sectors, and nearby social events give open doors to the two occupants and guests to interface, cultivating a feeling of brotherhood that characterizes the Kiwi lifestyle.

Outside Energy:

Sporting Pursuits:

The South Island's shocking scenes act as a characteristic jungle gym for outside lovers. In 2024, local people embrace the Kiwi love for sporting pursuits like climbing, cycling, kayaking, and skiing. From the lavish Abel Tasman Public Park to the blanketed pinnacles of the Southern Alps, the South Island offers assorted settings for open air undertakings.

Lawn bar-b-ques and Ocean side Days:

The Kiwi lifestyle frequently rotates around the outside, and patio grills and ocean side days are valued customs.

In 2024, guests can encounter the delight of imparting a dinner to loved ones in the midst of the beautiful scenery of the South Island's sea shores or moving slopes.

Culinary Joys:

New and Nearby Produce:

Kiwis invest heavily in their ranch to-table way to deal with food. In 2024, South Island markets and restaurants feature the overflow of new, privately obtained produce. From delicious sheep to fish luxuries, the Kiwi lifestyle praises the lavishness of New Zealand's culinary contributions.

Espresso Culture:

New Zealand's espresso culture is an indispensable piece of the Kiwi lifestyle. Bistros and high quality cafés are bountiful in towns and urban communities across the South Island, welcoming local people and guests the same to appreciate skillfully blended coffee while absorbing the casual climate.

Maintainability Practices:

Natural Cognizance:

Maintainability is profoundly imbued in the Kiwi ethos, and in 2024, this responsibility is apparent in different parts of day to day existence. From eco-accommodating facilities to local area drove preservation drives, the South Island embodies the Kiwi devotion to saving its unblemished common habitat.

Decreased Squander:

Kiwis effectively take part in squander decrease works on, including reusing and limiting single-use plastics. Economical residing isn't simply a pattern however a lifestyle that stretches out to residents decisions in their homes, working environments, and networks.

Expressions and Culture:

Imaginative Articulation:

The Kiwi lifestyle is enhanced by a flourishing expressions and culture scene. In 2024, guests can investigate neighborhood exhibitions, go to live exhibitions, and draw in with the dynamic imaginative local area. Maori craftsmanship, contemporary displays, and conventional exhibitions add to the social mosaic of the South Island.

Film and Writing:

New Zealand has a rich realistic and scholarly history, and the Kiwi lifestyle incorporates an affection for narrating. From investigating famous film areas to digging into crafted by neighborhood creators, guests can encounter the social account that shapes the character of the South Island.

Navigating the South Island

Gateway Cities: Christchurch, Dunedin, and Beyond

In 2024, the South Island of New Zealand remains an entryway to unrivaled normal excellence, social extravagance, and energetic metropolitan habitats.

Christchurch and Dunedin, two conspicuous urban communities, act as doors to the different marvels that lie past. As we set out on an excursion through these door urban communities and their environmental factors, we uncover the special encounters, social experiences, and normal wonders that characterize the South Island in 2024.

Christchurch: The Nursery City Rethought:

Recuperation and Recharging:

Christchurch, lovingly known as the Nursery City, has gone through an extraordinary excursion since the quakes of 2010 and 2011. In 2024, the city remains as a demonstration of strength and development, with a rethought metropolitan scene that flawlessly mixes current engineering with lavish vegetation.

Botanic Nurseries and Avon Waterway:

The core of Christchurch beats inside its Botanic Nurseries, a rambling desert garden of dynamic vegetation along the banks of the wandering Avon Stream. Drop-kicking along the stream or investigating the nurseries by foot or bike stays a quintessential Christchurch experience, offering quietness amid the metropolitan clamor.

Inventive Expressions Scene:
Christchurch's crafts and culture scene keeps on prospering with the presence of the Christchurch Workmanship Exhibition and the energetic road workmanship enhancing the city's walls. Guests in 2024 can observe the combination of conventional and contemporary articulations, mirroring the city's dynamic soul.

Dunedin: The Edinburgh of the South:
Structural Legacy:
Dunedin, frequently alluded to as the Edinburgh of the South, brags a structural scene suggestive of its Scottish legacy. The notable Otago Promontory, Victorian-period

structures, and the famous Dunedin Rail Route station give a brief look into the city's rich history.

Untamed life Experiences:

Past its metropolitan appeal, Dunedin fills in as a door to wonderful natural life encounters. In 2024, guests can leave on eco-accommodating visits to observe the uncommon yellow-looked-at penguins and the great gooney bird settlements that call the Otago Promontory home.

Understudy Energy:

Home to the College of Otago, New Zealand's most established college, Dunedin radiates a vivacious understudy environment. The city's energetic energy is reflected in its bistros, lively expressions scene, and the clamoring Octagon, a focal center for diversion and occasions.

Past the Passages: Investigating the South Island's Fortunes:

Aoraki/Mount Cook Public Park:

Leaving Christchurch, the excursion to Aoraki/Mount Cook Public Park unfurls a scene overwhelmed by New Zealand's most elevated top. Climbing trails, cold lakes, and all-encompassing vistas make this locale a sanctuary for outside fans and nature sweethearts.

Queenstown and Fiordland:

Wandering southwest from Dunedin prompts the experience capital of Queenstown. Encircled by the sensational scenes of Fiordland, this locale offers adrenaline junkies bungee bouncing, fly sailing, and climbing open doors amid the stunning fjords.

Abel Tasman Public Park:

Toward the north, past Christchurch, lies the Abel Tasman Public Park. Brilliant sea shores, turquoise waters, and waterfront trails coax guests to investigate the immaculate magnificence of this beachfront heaven.

Social and Culinary Encounters:

Neighborhood Food:

Both Christchurch and Dunedin are culinary centers, offering a different exhibit of eating encounters. In 2024, guests can enjoy ranch-to-table cooking, and relishing neighborhood luxuries and wines that grandstand the South Island's gastronomic ability.

Maori Social Drenching:

Past the metropolitan habitats, Maori social encounters are woven into the texture of the South Island. From directed voyages through customary marae to social exhibitions, guests can dive into the rich legacy of the native Maori individuals.

Supportable The travel industry Drives:

In 2024, both Christchurch and Dunedin epitomize New Zealand's obligation to manage the travel industry. Eco-accommodating facilities, protection drives, and mindful travel industry rehearses add to the conservation of the South Island's immaculate climate.

Transportation: From Picturesque Drives to Helicopter Rides

In 2024, navigating the enrapturing scenes of New Zealand's South Island is an experience in itself. From notable grand drives to thrilling helicopter rides, transportation choices unfurl an embroidery of encounters that reflect the different magnificence of the district. As we investigate the different ways of exploring the South Island, we should dig into the extensive and exceptional methods of transportation that characterize the excursion in 2024.

Beautiful Drives:
Milford Street:

Famous as one of the world's most beautiful drives, Milford Street takes explorers from Te Anau to Milford Sound, offering amazing perspectives on Fiordland's mountains, lakes, and rich woods. In 2024, an improved street framework guarantees a smooth and stunning excursion through this notorious course.

Arthur's Pass:

Interfacing the East and West Drifts, Arthur's Pass is a bumpy intersection encircled by a high landscape. The drive through this public park gives an all-encompassing exhibit of the Southern Alps, with potential open doors for short climbs to cascades and perspectives.

Waterfront Pacific Rail route:

For an extraordinary mix of transportation and view, the Waterfront Pacific Railroad runs between Christchurch and Picton, navigating the sensational seaside scenes of the South Island. In 2024, explorers can appreciate all-encompassing perspectives on the Pacific Sea and grape plantation-covered slopes from the solace of a picturesque train venture.

Helicopter Rides:

Fiordland Helicopter Visits:

Finding the remote corners of Fiordland Public Park turns into an exceptional involvement in helicopter visits. In 2024, guests can take off over the transcending tops, flowing cascades, and flawless fjords, acquiring a 10,000-foot viewpoint of this immaculate wild.

Aoraki/Mount Cook Helicopter Campaigns:

Helicopter campaigns around Aoraki/Mount Cook Public Park offer a dreamlike experience with New Zealand's most elevated top. Ice sheet arrivals and all-encompassing flights grandstand the snow-capped magnificence of the locale, making extraordinary minutes high over the Southern Alps.

Ship Intersections:

Interislander Ship:

Interfacing the North and South Islands, the Interislander Ship venture between Wellington and Picton is a picturesque oceanic experience. Cruising through the Marlborough Sounds, travelers in 2024 can partake in the amazing waterfront scenes and spot marine life during this beautiful intersection.

Lake Wakatipu Travels:

Queenstown, settled on the shores of Lake Wakatipu, offers quiet ship travel. In 2024, guests can appreciate comfortable boat rides on the lake, encompassed by the magnificence of the Remarkables mountain range and the beguiling lakeside town.

Electric Vehicle Investigation:

Eco-Accommodating Excursions:

By New Zealand's obligation to maintainability, electric vehicles are acquiring prevalence for investigating the South Island. The charging framework has extended, empowering eco-cognizant explorers to set out on travels with negligible natural effect, especially along the shocking West Coast.

Tesla Visits:

One of a kind toward the South Island, Tesla visits give an eco-accommodating and sumptuous method for investigating the scenes. In 2024, directed Tesla visits offer a mix of maintainability and solace, permitting explorers to see the value in the magnificence of the locale without leaving a carbon impression.

Cycling Undertakings:

Otago Focal Rail Trail:

For cycling devotees, the Otago Focal Rail Trail is a famous excursion through memorable gold mining scenes and beguiling country towns. In 2024, very much kept up with trails and bicycle cordial facilities make this cycling experience open and charming.

Queenstown Bicycle Trails:

Queenstown's broad organization of bicycle trails permits riders to investigate the lakeside, mountains, and encompassing valleys. From adrenaline-siphoning downhill paths to relaxed lakeside rides, Queenstown takes special care of cyclists, everything being equal, giving a novel point of view on the district's magnificence.

Practical Tips for Smooth Travels

You are setting out on an excursion to New Zealand's South Island in 2024 commitments spectacular scenes, social lavishness, and remarkable undertakings. To capitalize on your movements and guarantee a consistent encounter, it's fundamental to be good to go. This guide gives useful hints that will improve your excursion, covering angles from transportation and convenience to social subtleties and outside investigation.

Grasping the Climate:

Changed Environments:

The South Island flaunts different environments, going from the calm seaside locales to elevated regions. Pack appropriately, including layers for abrupt weather conditions changes, particularly assuming you intend to investigate waterfront and rugged regions.

Occasional Contemplations:

New Zealand's seasons are inverse to those in the Northern Side of the equator. Summer (December to February) offers a wonderful climate, while winter (June to August) carries snow toward the Southern Alps. Plan your visit given the exercises you wish to seek after.

Transportation Experiences:

Vehicle Rentals:

Think about leasing a vehicle to investigate the South Island at your speed. Streets are very much kept up with, and picturesque drives are a feature. Book ahead of time, particularly during top seasons, and be aware of driving on the left half of the street.

Public Transportation:

Use New Zealand's proficient public transportation organization, including transport and trains. The Beach Front Pacific Rail Line and Interislander Ship give tourist detours between Christchurch and Picton.

Homegrown Flights:

In the case of covering huge distances, homegrown flights are advantageous and time-effective. Territorial air terminals, like Queenstown and Dunedin, interface significant objections.

Convenience Techniques:

Various Choices:

From extravagant hotels to financial plan cordial lodgings, the South Island offers a scope of facilities. Book ahead of time, particularly during top traveler seasons, and investigate choices that line up with your inclinations and financial plan.

Special Stays:
Consider remaining in special facilities like store lodgings, ranch stays, or eco-accommodating hotels to upgrade your South Island experience.

Social Behavior:
Maori Good tidings:
Look into Maori customs, including the conventional hello called the hongi. This includes a squeezing of noses and implies a common breath of life.

Regarding Customs:
While visiting the marae (Maori meeting grounds), be conscious and follow social conventions. Look for consent before taking photographs and embrace the chance to find out about Maori legacy.

Outside Experience Tips:

Security Precautionary measures:

If participating in open-air exercises like climbing or water sports, focus on security. Take a look at weather patterns, illuminate somebody about your arrangements, and convey important gear, particularly in distant regions.

Natural life Experiences:

Regard natural life living spaces and keep a protected separation while noticing creatures, whether it's penguins on the Otago Landmass or seals on the West Coast.

Feasible The travel industry Practices:

Eco-Accommodating Decisions:

Embrace New Zealand's obligation to manageability by pursuing eco-accommodating decisions. Decide on facilities with green drives, limit plastic use, and comply with protection rules while investigating regular regions.

Social and Ecological Regard:

Be aware of the effect of your visit on both the climate and neighborhood networks. Follow Leave No Follow standards, support nearby organizations, and take part in mindful travel industry drives.

Money and Network:

Money Contemplations:

New Zealand utilizes the New Zealand Dollar (NZD). Illuminate your bank about your movement dates to stay away from any issues with credit/check card exchanges, and consider conveying some neighborhood money for more modest foundations.

Availability:

While significant urban communities have dependable web and versatile inclusion, a few far-off regions might have restricted networks. Consider buying a neighborhood SIM card or convenient Wi-Fi gadget if remaining associated is fundamental.

CHAPTER TWO

Southern Alps: Majestic Peaks and Adventure Awaits

Mount Cook National Park

Settled in the core of New Zealand's South Island, Mount Cook Public Park remains a demonstration of the country's unrivaled normal excellence. Home to the transcending pinnacles of the Southern Alps and delegated by the superb Aoraki/Mount Cook, the most noteworthy top in New Zealand, this public park offers a charming mix of high scenes, flawless icy masses, and an abundance of open-air undertakings. In 2024, the recreation area will be a sanctuary for nature fans, explorers, and those looking for a break into the immaculate wild.

Topography and Scene:

Mount Cook Public Park traverses more than 700 square kilometers and is important for the bigger UNESCO World Legacy recorded Te Wahipounamu region. The recreation area's scene is overwhelmed by the Southern Alps, with Aoraki/Mount Cook standing gladly at 3,724 meters. The recreation area brags a different reach conditions, from lavish rainforests in the lower valleys to ice sheets and extremely durable snowfields at higher heights.

Outstanding Highlights:

Aoraki/Mount Cook:

Aoraki/Mount Cook, the recreation area's namesake, is a magnet for mountain climbers and photographic artists the same. The tough excellence of its snow-shrouded tops and the encompassing glacial masses make it a notorious image of New Zealand's untamed wild.

Tasman Ice sheet:

The recreation area is home to the Tasman Ice Sheet, the longest icy mass in New Zealand. Guests can take boat visits to explore the terminal lake and witness the dazzling sight of ice sheets splitting away from the glacial mass.

Prostitute Valley Track:

Prestigious as one of New Zealand's greatest day climbs, the Prostitute Valley Track takes guests on an excursion through snow-capped knolls, over swing spans, lastly to the Whore Lake, where the impression of Aoraki/Mount Cook causes an entrancing situation.

Mueller Hovel:

For those looking for a really difficult experience, the Mueller Cottage offers a remunerating journey with staggering all-encompassing perspectives on the encompassing mountains. Dawn and dusk at the cottage give photographic artists an exceptional material of varieties.

Exercises and Entertainment:

Climbing and Slogging:

Mount Cook Public Park brags a broad organization of climbing trails reasonable for all degrees of explorers. From short strolls to multi-day hikes, the recreation area offers amazing chances to investigate its different environments.

Elevated Climbing:

Aoraki/Mount Cook draws in prepared climbers from around the world. Getting over campaigns range from moderately clear risings to testing specialized gets over, giving a different scope of choices for mountain climbers.

Stargazing:

The recreation area is assigned as a Worldwide Dim Sky Hold, making it an ideal spot for stargazing. On starry evenings, guests are blessed to receive an amazing showcase of the southern half of the globe's heavenly miracles.

Preservation and Maintainability:

Mount Cook Public Park puts major areas of strength for preservation, meaning saving its novel biological systems and biodiversity. Manageable the travel industry rehearses are urged to limit the effect on the fragile high climate, guaranteeing that people in the future can keep on partaking in this flawless wild.

Queenstown and the Remarkables

Settled on the shores of Lake Wakatipu, encompassed by grand mountains, Queenstown remains a gem in New Zealand's South Island. In 2024, this pleasant location keeps on enamoring explorers with its dazzling scenes, experience exercises, and an extraordinary mix of regular magnificence and metropolitan appeal. Among the striking highlights that make Queenstown uncommon are the notorious Remarkables mountain range, a jungle gym for open-air fans, and a wellspring of motivation for craftsmen and nature sweethearts the same.

Queenstown: A Lakeside Sanctuary

Queenstown, frequently alluded to as the "Experience Capital of the World," is famous for its different scope of sporting exercises and stunning landscape. The town, with its enchanting roads, energetic culture, and inviting climate, fills in as an ideal passage to investigate the marvels of the South Island.

Experience Capital:

Queenstown's standing as the experience capital is merited, offering plenty of adrenaline-siphoning exercises, for example, bungee bouncing, skydiving, and stream drifting.

In 2024, new and imaginative experience encounters have arisen, guaranteeing that daredevils track down clever ways of testing themselves against the setting of Queenstown's staggering scenes.

Beautiful Magnificence:

Lake Wakatipu, molded like a lightning bolt, is the focal point of Queenstown. Guests can take beautiful travels or relaxed walks around the waterfront to ingest the excellence of the completely clear lake against the scenery of the encompassing mountains.

Culinary Joys

Queenstown flaunts a different culinary scene, offering all that from high-end food to road food. In 2024, new gastronomic encounters have arisen, mixing neighborhood flavors with worldwide impacts, making it a heaven for food lovers.

The Remarkables: Superb Pinnacles and Snow-capped Experiences

The Remarkables mountain range, appropriately named for its amazing view, remains a notorious background to Queenstown. This reach is an all-year objective, offering exercises for each season.

Winter Wonderland:

The Remarkables are a sanctuary for winter sports fans. The ski fields, furnished with cutting-edge offices, draw skiers and snowboarders looking for flawless slants and stunning displays.

In 2024, upgrades in the foundation and extra snowmaking abilities guarantee an improved winter insight, making it an optimal objective for the two amateurs and prepared high aficionados.

Summer Departures:

As the snow dissolves, the Remarkables change into a jungle gym for explorers, mountain bikers, and nature sweethearts. Trails wander through high knolls, offering shocking vistas of the encompassing valleys and lakes.

Eco-Accommodating Drives:

In arrangement with New Zealand's obligation to natural maintainability, the Remarkables have executed eco-accommodating drives to protect the sensitive elevated environment. Guests can now partake in the excellence of the area while adding to its safeguarding.

Hiking Trails and Alpine Escapades

In 2024, New Zealand's South Island entices explorers with plenty of climbing trails and elevated ventures that feature the island's stunning scenes, from snow-covered tops to rich valleys. This far-reaching guide welcomes you to find the most remarkable climbing trails, giving bits of knowledge into the normal marvels, social encounters, and outside experiences that anticipate the core of Aotearoa.

Aoraki/Mount Cook Public Park:

Whore Valley Track:

This famous path offers a dazzling excursion through the Prostitute Valley, driving climbers to the terminal lake with all-encompassing perspectives on Aoraki/Mount Cook. In 2024, the redesigned framework guarantees a protected and charming experience, and directed visits give bits of knowledge into the locale's regular history.

Mueller Cabin Course:

For additional accomplished climbers looking for a high test, the Mueller Cottage Course rises through snow-capped knolls and scree inclines to a mountain cabin with unmatched perspectives on Aoraki/Mount Cook and the Southern Alps.

Fiordland Public Park:

Milford Track:

Frequently alluded to as the "best stroll on the planet," the Milford Track is a 53-kilometer venture through Fiordland's flawless wild. In 2024, explorers can navigate valleys, cross high passes, and witness glorious cascades, coming full circle in a boat voyage on Milford Sound.

Routeburn Track:

Interfacing Fiordland and Mount Hopeful Public Stops, the Routeburn Track is a different path through elevated glades, beech timberlands, and mountain ranges. Amazing vistas of the Hollyford Valley and Lake Mackenzie anticipate explorers on this multi-day experience.

Southern Alps:

Kepler Track:

Circumnavigating the Kepler Mountains, this 60-kilometer circle gives explorers a vivid involvement with Fiordland Public Park. In 2024, the Kepler Track offers different scenes, from beech backwoods to subalpine zones, and all-encompassing perspectives on Lake Te Anau and encompassing pinnacles.

Nelson Lakes Public Park:

The Nelson Lakes locale acquaints explorers with elevated lakes and tough mountains. The Travers-Sabine Circuit, a multi-day journey, surrounds Lake Rotoiti, introducing potential chances to observe different vegetation, birdlife, and glaciated valleys.

West Coast Ice sheets:

Franz Josef Ice sheet Valley Walk:

Ideal for those looking for a more limited trip, the Franz Josef Ice Sheet Valley Walk takes explorers to the terminal essence of the icy mass. Witness the leftovers of the last ice age and wonder about the unique scene etched by ice and time.

Copland Track:

For a more vivid elevated insight, the Copland Track on the West Coast investigates the Copland Valley, offering looks at icy masses, hot pools, and all-encompassing vistas of the Southern Alps.

Arthur's Pass Public Park:

Torrential slide Pinnacle Track:

Arthur's Pass Public Park flaunts the difficult yet remunerating Torrential slide Pinnacle Track. Rise to the highest point for clearing perspectives on the Southern Alps, Waimakariri Valley, and the Canterbury Fields.

Otira Valley Track:

This valley track in Arthur's Pass leads explorers through lavish rainforests, uncovering flowing cascades, before climbing to a high bowl with shocking perspectives on the encompassing pinnacles.

Security and Arrangement:

Climate Mindfulness:

New Zealand's weather conditions can be erratic. Take a look at conjectures before leaving on climbs, and be ready for unexpected changes in conditions, particularly in high regions.

Hardware Basics:

Pack basics, including strong climbing boots, a waterproof dress, a medical aid unit, and route devices. For longer journeys, guarantee you have adequate food, water, and crisis supplies.

Cabin Reservations:

On the off chance of arranging multi-day climbs with cottage facilities, think about reserving a spot ahead of time, particularly during top seasons. The Division of Preservation (DOC) oversees a significant number of these offices.

Mirror-Like Lakes and Crystal Clear Waters

Lake Tekapo: Stargazing Haven

Settled amid the staggering scenes of New Zealand's South Island, Lake Tekapo stands as a pleasant frigid lake as well as a divine haven for stargazers. In 2024, Lake Tekapo keeps on charming guests with its completely clear skies, unmatched heavenly perspectives, and a pledge to safeguard the regular magnificence that makes it a stargazing sanctuary like no other. Go along with us on an excursion to investigate the heavenly marvels that are anticipated at Lake Tekapo, where the universe and Earth combine in a stunning dance.

Astro-The travel industry at Lake Tekapo:

Worldwide Dull Sky Hold:

Lake Tekapo holds the esteemed title of being essential for the Aoraki Mackenzie Worldwide Dim Sky Save, one of the biggest such saves internationally. In 2024, the save's obligation to limit light contamination guarantees an unmatched stargazing experience.

Tekapo's Dull Sky Task:

The Dim Sky Venture, based at Lake Tekapo, keeps on being a point of convergence for the travel industry. With best-in-class observatories, planetariums, and master stargazing visits, guests can dig into the miracles of the southern side of the equator's night sky.

Stargazing Areas of Interest:

Mount John Observatory:

Roosted on Mount John, the observatory at Lake Tekapo offers all-encompassing perspectives on the encompassing scenes by day and an unhampered perspective on the night sky around evening time. In 2024, directed visits and public stargazing meetings give an understanding of the universe.

Church of the Great Shepherd:

The notorious Church of the Great Shepherd, with its genuine outline against the lake and mountains, turns into a divine signal around evening time. Stargazers frequently accumulate here to observe the Smooth Way angling across the sky.

Tekapo's Special Divine Highlights:

Southern Lights (Aurora Australis):

Lake Tekapo is an ideal spot for getting a brief look at the Southern Lights. In 2024, as sun-powered movement tops, guests get the opportunity to observe the entrancing dance of varieties across the southern skies.

Brilliant Evenings and Clear Skies:

Lake Tekapo's high-elevation area and fresh, clear air add to the excellent permeability of stars, planets, and divine peculiarities. The shortfall of light contamination improves the splendor of the night sky.

Heavenly Exercises and Encounters:

Stargazing Visits:

Joining a stargazing visit at Lake Tekapo is an unquestionable necessity. Learned guides utilize strong telescopes to divulge the secrets of far-off cosmic systems, planets, and groups of stars, giving an instructive and remarkable experience.

Night Sky Photography:

Photography fans can catch the heavenly display over Lake Tekapo's scenes. In 2024, photography studios and visits take special care of those looking to deify the magnificence of the night sky.

Facilities and Dim Sky-Accommodating Practices:

Dim Sky Facilities:

Lake Tekapo offers facilities that focus on dim sky-accommodating practices. From lodges with private observatories to store inns intended for ideal stargazing, guests can expand their divine insight into their visit.

Outside Underground aquifers:

Tekapo's outside natural aquifers give an extraordinary chance to stargaze while drenched in warm waters. Loosen up under the twilight sky, partaking in the serenity and excellence of the universe.

Stargazing Occasions and Celebrations:

Tekapo Starlight Celebration:

The Tekapo Starlight Celebration, held yearly, unites stargazers, astrophotographers, and devotees. In 2024, this celebration offers talks, studios, and night sky festivities, making it an optimal opportunity to encounter Lake Tekapo's heavenly miracles.

Meteor Showers and Heavenly Occasions:

Watch out for the galactic schedule for meteor showers, shrouds, and other heavenly occasions that beautify the skies above Lake Tekapo. Joining individual devotees during these peculiarities improves the feeling of the local area and shared wonder.

Wanaka's Quiet Magnificence

Settled on the shores of Lake Wanaka in the South Island of New Zealand, Wanaka remains a safe house of quietness, offering an exceptional mix of normal magnificence and outside undertakings. In 2024, Wanaka keeps on captivating guests with its tranquil scenes, unblemished lakeshores, and beguiling snow-capped town environment. From the magnificent Southern Alps to the clear waters of Lake Wanaka, this pure objective welcomes explorers to drench themselves in nature's peacefulness.

Geology and Scene:

Wanaka is arranged in the Otago area, encompassed by the Southern Alps and the immaculate waters of Lake Wanaka. The actual town radiates a casual energy, with a setting of snow-covered pinnacles and rich plant life. The vicinity of Mount Hopeful Public Park further upgrades Wanaka's allure, making it an entryway to some of New Zealand's most dazzling elevated landscape.

Eminent Elements:

Lake Wanaka:

The highlight of Wanaka, Lake Wanaka, is a cold lake prestigious for its unmistakable, dark blue waters. Guests can partake in a comfortable walk around the lakefront, take a boat journey, or have a go at kayaking to see the value in the stunning perspectives on the encompassing mountains completely.

Roy's Pinnacle Track:

A climb up Roy's Pinnacle is an unquestionable requirement for those looking for all-encompassing perspectives on Lake Wanaka and the Southern Alps. The path winds through elevated knolls, offering a remunerating challenge finishing in a famous perspective.

Perplexing World:

For a dash of peculiar tomfoolery, Wanaka is home to Perplexing World, a whimsical fascination highlighting mind-blowing optical deceptions, a monster labyrinth, and a bewildering bistro. It's a superb redirection for families and those with a lively soul.

Lavender Homesteads:

In the mid-year months, Wanaka's lavender homesteads burst into lively variety. A visit to these fragrant fields gives a tangible encounter and shocking photograph open doors against the scenery of the Southern Alps.

Exercises and Amusement:

Water Sports:

Lake Wanaka offers a jungle gym for water fans. Guests can participate in kayaking, paddleboarding, or take a picturesque boat voyage to investigate the secret straights and bays that spot the lake's shores.

Skiing and Snow Sports:

In the colder time of year, Wanaka changes into a frigid wonderland. The close by ski resorts, like Cardrona and High Pitch Cone, take care of the two amateurs and experienced skiers, offering unblemished slants and shocking snow-capped landscapes.

Wine sampling:

The Focal Otago wine area, eminent for its Pinot Noir, is effectively available from Wanaka. Wine fans can set out on a tasting visit to relish the kinds of the district while partaking in the pleasant grape plantation scenes.

Local Area and Culture:

Wanaka's modest community beguile is portrayed by an affectionate local area and a pledge to protect its normal legacy. Nearby business sectors, workmanship exhibitions, and local area occasions furnish guests with a chance to interface with the district's rich culture and agreeable local people.

The Allure of Fiordland

Settled in the southwestern corner of New Zealand's South Island, Fiordland allures with its untamed magnificence, emotional scenes, and a quality of peacefulness that dazzles the spirit. In 2024, this immaculate wild keeps on charming explorers, offering a vivid involvement with quite possibly of the most staggering and immaculate areas on The planet.

Magnificent Inlets:

Fiordland is eminent for its amazing coves, cut by old glacial masses. Milford Sound and Dicey Sound, the most well-known among them, feature sheer bluffs, flowing cascades, and completely clear waters. In 2024, endeavors to save the natural equilibrium of these coves have strengthened, guaranteeing that guests can wonder about their pristine loftiness.

Milford Sound: A Characteristic Miracle:

Milford Sound stands as the crown gem of Fiordland. Guests can leave on picturesque travels through the sound, passing famous milestones like Miter Pinnacle and Stirling Falls. In 2024, manageable travel industry drives have been carried out to safeguard the fragile marine biological system, considering a vivid encounter while saving the regular environment.

Dicey Sound: The Sound of Quiet:

Far-fetched Sound, known for its serenity and segregation, offers a more disconnected encounter. Open through a boating venture across Lake Manapouri and a transport ride over Wilmot Pass, this inlet furnishes a personal association with nature. In 2024, directed visits with an accentuation on protection training guarantee that guests leave with a profound appreciation for the area's biological significance.

Untamed life Experiences:

Fiordland is a shelter for natural-life devotees. Guests can detect fur seals, dolphins, and an assortment of bird animal categories, including the interesting Fiordland Peaked Penguin. Preservation endeavors in 2024 plan to safeguard these species, with eco-accommodating visit administrators giving educational encounters that feature the significance of protecting the district's biodiversity.

Slogging in Fiordland Public Park:

Fiordland Public Park, a UNESCO World Legacy site, is a heaven for explorers and nature sweethearts. The prestigious Milford Track and Kepler Track wind through old timberlands, elevated glades, and unblemished lakes, offering a vivid involvement with the core of Fiordland. In 2024, overhauled trail offices and improved interpretive signage enhance the slogging experience.

Stargazing in the Wild:

Fiordland's distant area and insignificant light contamination make it an optimal setting for stargazing. In 2024, astrotourism drives have built up some decent forward movement, furnishing guests with the chance to observe the southern half of the globe's divine marvels while encompassed by the immaculate magnificence of Fiordland.

West Coast Wonders

Pancake Rocks and Punakaiki

In 2024, the South Island of New Zealand keeps on enthralling explorers with its one-of-a-kind topographical marvels, and among them stands Punakaiki's Flapjack Rocks — a surprising waterfront development that challenges clarification. Settled on the rough west coast, Punakaiki coaxes explorers and nature lovers to observe the stunning excellence of nature's engineering. Go along with us on an excursion to investigate the enrapturing Flapjack Rocks and Punakaiki, where the powers of the

Tasman Ocean meet the old limestone bluffs in a tremendous showcase.

Development and Topographical Wonder:

Limestone Stacks and Blowholes:

The Flapjack Rocks are a progression of limestone developments looking like stacked hotcakes, shaped more than a huge number of years by the gathering of marine animals and flotsam and jetsam. These extraordinary stacks are supplemented by blowholes, which eject seawater in musical blasts during elevated tides and blustery climates.

Antiquated Limestone:

The stones' particular layering, similar to the layers of flapjacks, is a consequence of exchanging hard and delicate layers of limestone. The disintegration cycle over hundreds of years has shaped these developments, making a characteristic miracle that is both captivating and outwardly staggering.

Access and Trails:

Punakaiki Beach Front Track:

In 2024, the Punakaiki Beach front Track offers a superb climbing experience for those hoping to investigate the Flapjack Rocks and the encompassing shore. The very much kept up with trail gives all-encompassing perspectives on the Tasman Ocean and rich local vegetation.

Hotcake Rocks Walkway:

For a nearer experience with the Hotcake Shakes, the short Flapjack Rocks Walkway is open from the principal guest focus. This very much-planned way permits guests to wander through local seaside greenery and gives different review stages to a very close gander at the land ponders.

Flowing Display:

Elevated Tide Wonder:

The wizardry of Punakaiki unfurls during the elevated tide, particularly during a blustery climate when the Tasman Ocean floods against the precipices. The blowholes emit marvelous presentations, shooting seawater up high and making a tactile ensemble of sound and fog.

Tide Timings:

Guests ought to take a look at the tide timings to upgrade their experience. Elevated tide upgrades the blowhole shows, while low tide offers an opportunity to investigate the stone developments near the ocean.

Guest Center and Translation:

Flapjack Rocks and Punakaiki Guest Center:

The very designated guest place gives important data about the topographical cycles that molded the Hotcake Rocks. Intuitive presentations and proficient staff offer bits of knowledge about the vegetation, fauna, and social history of the area.

Directed Visits:

Directed visits, accessible in 2024, give top-to-bottom information about the normal and social meaning of Punakaiki. Neighborhood guides share tales about the Māori legends related to the district and the exceptional biodiversity that flourishes in this waterfront climate.

Facilities and Nearby Food:

Punakaiki Facilities:

In 2024, Punakaiki offers a scope of facilities, from comfortable hotels to ocean-side retreats, permitting guests to drench themselves in the beachfront mood. Consider remaining for the time being to encounter the quiet magnificence of the region after the jet-setters have withdrawn.

Nearby Feasting:

Punakaiki flaunts enchanting bistros and eateries serving new, privately obtained cooking. Enjoy fish treats while partaking in the dusk over the Tasman Ocean for a vivid encounter.

Economical The travel industry Practices:

Preservation Drives:

In 2024, Punakaiki stresses maintaining the travel industry practices to safeguard its regular magnificence. Preservation endeavors incorporate safeguarding local greenery, limiting the ecological effect of the travel industry, and teaching guests about capable travel.

Local area Commitment:

The nearby local area effectively takes part in the protection of the area. Drives, for example, ocean-side clean-ups and instructive projects add to the continuous insurance of Punakaiki's special biological systems.

Fox and Franz Josef Glaciers

Settled inside the enamoring scenes of New Zealand's South Island, the Fox and Franz Josef Ice sheets stand as frozen wonders, drawing explorers and nature devotees the same. In 2024, these glacial masses keep on directing consideration with their sensational ice developments, rough landscape, and special availability. The Fox and Franz Josef Glacial masses, both situated in Westland Tai Poutini Public Park, offer a brief look into the unique excellence of the Southern Alps.

Geology and Development:

Franz Josef Glacial mass:

The Franz Josef Glacial mass slips from the Southern Alps to only 240 meters above ocean level, making it one of the steepest and quickest-moving glacial masses on the planet. Its dynamic nature, continually moving and streaming, makes an entrancing scene of ice caverns, chasms, and seracs.

Fox Icy mass:

Neighboring the Franz Josef Ice sheet, the Fox Icy mass flaunts a comparative sensational plunge from the Southern Alps. It is known for its momentous length, extending north of 13 kilometers, and its lower rise takes into consideration a one-of-a-kind cold experience amid a rich rainforest.

Remarkable Elements:

Ice Caverns and Chasms:

The glacial masses are embellished with mind-boggling ice arrangements, including staggering ice caverns and profound precipices. Directed visits give a protected and exciting method for investigating these regular miracles, offering guests an opportunity to observe the frigid scene very closely.

Heli-Climbing and Ice Climbing:

Courageous spirits can take to the skies on a helicopter visit that terrains on the ice sheet, giving a selective chance to directed climbs and ice climbing. The ethereal viewpoint uncovers the boundlessness of the icy masses and the encompassing elevated landscape.

Te Wahipounamu:

Both Fox and Franz Josef Icy masses are important for Te Wahipounamu, a UNESCO World Legacy site known for its excellent regular highlights and Maori social importance. The icy masses are indispensable parts of this safeguarded region, underlining their natural significance.

Hot Pools at Franz Josef:

Following a day of investigation, guests can loosen up in the restoring hot pools at Franz Josef. Settled in a rainforest setting, these warm pools offer a quiet retreat with perspectives on the encompassing mountains.

Manageability and Preservation:

Endeavors to offset the travel industry with protection are principal in the Fox and Franz Josef Ice sheets locale. Directed visits comply with severe ecological rules, and drives are set up to safeguard the fragile biological systems encompassing the ice sheets, guaranteeing that people in the future can keep on wondering about these regular marvels.

Climate and Availability:

While weather patterns can be flighty, 2024 keeps on seeing a scope of direct visits that adjust to the icy mass' powerful climate. Helicopter flights and climbs offer a novel mix of experience and well-being, permitting guests to encounter the icy masses no matter what the climate.

Coastal Magic: Greymouth to Haast

Set out on a hypnotizing venture along the tough West Shoreline of New Zealand's South Island, where untamed normal magnificence meets the powerful Tasman Ocean. In 2024, the waterfront stretch from Greymouth to Haast keeps on winding around its spell on explorers, offering an unmatched mix of emotional scenes, rich Maori history, and credible Kiwi friendliness.

Greymouth: Entryway to the Wild West Coast:

Settled at the mouth of the Dim Stream, Greymouth fills in as the ideal beginning stage for this waterfront experience. In 2024, the town holds its appeal, mixing memorable importance with present-day conveniences. Guests can investigate Monteith's Brewery, enjoy neighborhood cooking, and find out about the town's gold mining legacy at Shantytown.

Punakaiki's Flapjack Rocks and Blowholes:

A short drive south from Greymouth prompts Punakaiki, where the celebrated Hotcake Rocks and Blowholes anticipate. In 2024, raised walkways and survey stages give improved points of view of these limestone developments, displaying the strong powers of nature that have shaped this seaside wonder.

Hokitika: Jade Capital of New Zealand:

Hokitika, eminent for its high-quality jade (pounamu) cutting, welcomes guests to observe the making of customary Maori treasures. In 2024, the town's imaginative local area has thrived, offering a much more prominent exhibit of the novel, carefully assembled keepsakes.

Franz Josef and Fox Icy Masses:

Going on the south, the West Coast uncovers the lofty Franz Josef and Fox Icy masses. In 2024, the travel industry will guarantee that guests can in any case wonder about these normal miracles while regarding the sensitive environment. Helicopter visits and directed climbs give amazing perspectives on the icy scenes.

Untamed life Experiences at Lake Matheson:

Lake Matheson, close to Fox Glacial mass, is well known for its intelligent waters offering dazzling mirror-like perspectives on Aoraki/Mount Cook and Mount Tasman. In 2024, eco-accommodating visits accentuate the conservation of the lake's immaculate climate, permitting guests to see the value in the excellence of the Southern Alps reflected in its actual waters.

Haast: Entryway to the World Legacy Region:

The excursion finishes in Haast, a humble community that fills in as the doorway toward the Westland Tai Poutini Public Park World Legacy Region. In 2024, Haast will be a center point for investigating the locale's different biological systems, including rainforests, mountains, and seaside environments.

Connoisseur Encounters:

All through this beachfront odyssey, gastronomic pleasures are anticipated. From Greymouth's fish rarities to Hokitika's high-quality chocolates, the West Coast offers a different culinary encounter. In 2024, nearby diners keep on enhancing and consolidating new, privately obtained fixings into their menus.

CHAPTER THREE

Encountering the Maori Spirit

Maori Cultural Centers and Performances

New Zealand's South Island is a gold mine of regular magnificence, and settled inside its shocking scenes are dynamic Maori social focuses that feature the rich legacy of the native Maori individuals. In 2024, these social centers keep on enamoring guests with vivid encounters, customary exhibitions, and a profound plunge into the old traditions that have formed the character of the Maori people group.

Te Dad o Te Waipounamu: The Heartbeat of Maori Culture
At the core of the South Island's social scene lies Te Daddy o Te Waipounamu, a Maori social focus that fills in as a living demonstration of the customs and

accounts of the Ngai Tahu iwi, the biggest Maori clan in the South Island. The middle is a powerful mix of contemporary and customary components, offering guests a shrewd excursion into the Ngai Tahu legacy.

Inside Te Father o Te Waipounamu, intelligent shows welcome visitors to investigate Maori cosmology, the meaning of tribal scenes, and the profound association with the land. Educated guides share stories that went down through ages, giving a significant comprehension of the Maori lifestyle.

Aoraki Bound: A Vivid Social Excursion

For those looking for a more vivid encounter, Aoraki Bound remains a remarkable chance to draw in Maori culture in the core of the Southern Alps. This social experience program joins open-air exercises with customary Maori works, encouraging a profound association among members and the climate.

Aoraki Bound offers a comprehensive way to deal with understanding Maori customs, integrating exercises, for example, waka rowing, bramble basic instincts, and star route. Members witness social exhibitions as well as effectively partake in them, making recollections that rise above the limits of customary the travel industry.

Te Waipounamu Maori Social Celebration: Observing Variety

In 2024, the Te Waipounamu Maori Social Celebration becomes the overwhelming focus, uniting different Maori people groups from across the South Island. This lively festival features the uniqueness of every clan's social articulation, from the strong haka to the smooth poi dance.

The celebration gives a stage for Maori specialists, narrators, and entertainers to share their gifts and stories. Participants have the chance to enjoy conventional Maori food, take part in craftsmanship studios, and take part in significant discussions with local area pioneers, encouraging a feeling of solidarity and appreciation for the variety inside Maori culture.

Kaiapoi Dad: Protecting Antiquated Customs

In the memorable town of Kaiapoi, the Kaiapoi Dad fills in as a social fortress, safeguarding the old practices of the Ngai Tahu individuals. This braced town offers directed visits that dive into the meaning of dad destinations, the craft of cutting, and the otherworldly practices implanted in Maori culture.

Guests to Kaiapoi Dad witness live showings of customary specialties, including the complicated specialty of ta moko (inking) and whakairo (cutting). The experience cultivates a profound appreciation for the abilities that went down through the ages, stressing the significance of social protection despite current difficulties.

Conventional Maori Cooking

New Zealand's South Island isn't just famous for its stunning scenes yet in addition for its rich socially woven artwork, including the lively culinary customs of the Maori public. In 2024, the conventional Maori food of the South Island keeps on enrapturing local people and guests the same, offering an extraordinary mix of native fixings, cooking techniques, and social importance. We should dig into the different and delightful universe of customary Maori cooking, encountering the quintessence of New Zealand's South Island through its food.

Kai Maori: The Culinary Articulation of Maori Culture

Kai Maori Reasoning: Vital to Maori cooking is the idea of "Kai," which includes food, food, and the demonstration of sharing. Kai Maori mirrors the profound association between the Maori public and the land, stressing supportability and regard for nature.

Fixings: The South Island's customary Maori dishes highlight a variety of privately obtained fixings, including kumara (yam), puha (a local verdant green), koura (freshwater crawfish), and paua (abalone), displaying the district's different biological systems.

Hangi: A Respected Cooking Technique

Cooking Strategy: One of the most notorious parts of Maori food is the Hangi, a conventional earth stove. This cooking technique includes digging a pit in the ground, warming stones, and afterward layering food (meat, vegetables, and at times fish) on top. The pit is covered with earth, permitting the food to slow-cook in its juices.

Culinary Occasions: In 2024, Hangi encounters have advanced past conventional family social events. Numerous eateries and social focuses now offer Hangi feasts, giving an open door to local people and sightseers to partake in this old culinary custom.

Fish Delights: Embracing the Abundance of the Sea

Paua Wastes: Paua, a kind of abalone, has become the overwhelming focus in numerous Maori fish dishes.

Paua wastes, a famous delicacy, exhibit the rich kinds of this shellfish, frequently matched with native spices and flavors.

Whitebait Wastes: A South Island forte, whitebait squanders feature the district's plentiful freshwater assets. These little, clear fish are blended in with eggs and softly seared, making a fragile and flavorful treat.

Kawakawa and Horopito: Native Flavors

Homegrown Implantations: The South Island's Maori food depends intensely on local spices like kawakawa and horopito. These spices implant dishes with novel flavors and therapeutic properties, adding profundity to customary recipes.

Rongoa Maori: Past culinary purposes, kawakawa and horopito are esteemed in Rongoa Maori, conventional Maori medication. Their incorporation into cooking features the all-encompassing methodology the Maori take towards food and prosperity.

Current Understandings: Combination of Custom and Advancement

Contemporary Gourmet experts: In 2024, gourmet specialists in the South Island are joining conventional Maori fixings and cooking procedures with current culinary techniques. This combination safeguards the quintessence of Maori food as well as acquaints it with a more extensive crowd.

Ranch-to-Table Drives: The accentuation on maintainable and privately obtained fixings lines up with worldwide food patterns. Numerous cafés are taking on ranch to-table works, fashioning associations with nearby Maori people groups and displaying the genuineness of their dishes.

Marae Visits and Cultural Etiquette

New Zealand's South Island is a mother lode of rich Maori culture and custom, with marae visits giving an exceptional open door to guests to submerge themselves in the native lifestyle. As you set out on your excursion through this beautiful district in 2024, understanding the traditions and behavior encompassing marae visits is vital for a deferential and enhancing experience.

Grasping the Marae:

A marae is a holy and collective gathering ground, frequently filling in as the point of convergence for Maori social, social, and otherworldly exercises. It is where hereditary spirits are respected, and local area bonds are reinforced. While arranging a visit to a marae, it is crucial for look for consent from the nearby iwi (clan) and stick to the laid-out conventions.

Getting Consent:

Prior to going to a marae, it is standard to look for consent from the nearby iwi. This includes reaching the ancestral seniors or an assigned delegate to communicate your aim to visit and demand their approval. This motion exhibits regard for Maori customs and guarantees a warm greeting upon appearance.

Conventional Good tidings (Powhiri):

After coming to the marae, guests are customarily invited through a service known as a powhiri. This includes a progression of customs, including the karanga (calling) by the ladies, whaikorero (discourses) by the two hosts and guests, and the trading of hongi (squeezing noses together) as an image of solidarity. It is critical to follow the lead of your hosts during these customs and answer with modesty and appreciation.

Koha (Gift Giving):

Bringing a koha, or a gift, is a standard practice while visiting a marae. This offering represents appreciation for the friendliness stretched out by the hosts. It is fitting to talk about suitable koha choices with your hosts or look for direction from neighborhood sources to guarantee your gift lines up with social standards.

Regarding Tapu and Noa:

Maori culture puts incredible significance on the ideas of tapu (sacrosanct) and noa (conventional). Certain region of the marae might be considered tapu and untouchable to guests. It is pivotal to regard these limits and look for direction from your hosts to guarantee you explore the marae with responsiveness.

Social Responsiveness:

In all associations, social responsiveness is vital. Try not to hinder talks, keep a calm and deferential disposition, and shun participating in unseemly way of behaving. Photography and recording might be limited, so consistently look for consent prior to catching any minutes.

Taking part in Exercises:

Marae visits frequently incorporate different social exercises, for example, kapa haka (conventional execution expressions) and customary games. While investment is empowered, it is fundamental to heed the direction of your hosts and show energy without appropriating or slighting the social meaning of these practices.

Urban Vibes: Cities and Towns

Christchurch: Gardens and Resilience

In 2024, Christchurch, the biggest city in New Zealand's South Island, remains as a demonstration of strength, resurrection, and the agreeable concurrence of metropolitan existence with nature. Embracing a lively mix of innovation and custom, Christchurch has re-imagined itself following the quakes of 2010 and 2011, changing into a city that flourishes as well as flaunts dazzling nurseries and green spaces. Go along with us on an excursion to investigate Christchurch's thriving nurseries and the dauntless soul that characterizes the city in 2024.

Botanic Nurseries: A Green Desert Garden:

Notable Importance:

Christchurch's Botanic Nurseries, laid out in 1863, stay a green gem. In 2024, these nurseries grandstand a rich embroidery of vegetation, legacy trees, and blossoming botanical shows that draw local people and guests the same.

Avon Waterway Quietness:

The Botanic Nurseries' area along the wandering Avon Stream makes a quiet climate. Guests can appreciate drop-kicking along the stream or relaxed walks around themed gardens, including the Rose Nursery, Spice Nursery, and Water Nursery.

Protection and Biodiversity:

Christchurch's obligation to ecological supportability is apparent in the Botanic Nurseries. Protection drives, local plant shows, and instructive projects add to the conservation of biodiversity.

Christchurch Tremor Remembrance: Reflection and Strength:

Ōtautahi - Christchurch Tremor Remembrance:

The Ōtautahi - Christchurch Tremor Remembrance fills in as a piercing sign of the city's versatility even with misfortune. In 2024, guests can think about the effect of the seismic tremors while valuing the imaginativeness and imagery of the dedication.

Recovery and Remaking:

Christchurch's post-seismic tremor recreation has been set apart by imaginative design and metropolitan preparation. In 2024, the cityscape features a mix of contemporary designs and reestablished legacy structures, showing the local area's obligation to renewal.

Mona Vale: Polish in Legacy:

Memorable Property and Nurseries:

Mona Vale, an exquisite noteworthy estate encompassed by manicured gardens, gives a retreat in the core of Christchurch. In 2024, the nurseries exhibit a mix of local and outlandish plantings, while the residence offers a brief look into the city's past.

Rose Nursery Quality:

The Mona Vale Rose Nursery is a feature, bragging a different assortment of roses in full blossom. Guests can meander through the fragrant ways, appreciating the magnificence of this fastidiously kept garden.

Christchurch's Road Workmanship Scene: Articulation and Inventiveness:

Dynamic Road Workmanship Area:

As a result of the seismic tremors, Christchurch embraced road craftsmanship as a type of articulation and renewal. In 2024, the city's dynamic road workmanship scene keeps on advancing, with laneways and structures embellished with beautiful wall paintings, mirroring the strength and imagination of the local area.

Range Road Workmanship Celebration:

The Range Road Workmanship Celebration, held consistently, changes the city into an outside display. Guests in 2024 can investigate new establishments, go to studios, and witness the extraordinary force of public craftsmanship in metropolitan spaces.

Riccarton House and Shrub: Authentic Appeal and Regular Magnificence:

Legacy House and Gardens:

Riccarton House, a notable property encompassed by sweeping nurseries, offers a brief look into nineteenth-century provincial life. In 2024, guests can investigate the carefully safeguarded house and meander through the nurseries, which highlight a blend of local and colorful plantings.

Shrubbery Strolls and Birdlife:

Riccarton Hedge, neighboring the estate, is an interesting leftover of local timberland. Nature devotees can leave on shrub strolls, experiencing local vegetation and birdlife inside the core of Christchurch.

Local area Nurseries and Maintainable Practices:

Shared Spaces for Developing:

Christchurch embraces local area gardens, where inhabitants meet up to develop plants and fabricate a feeling of the local area. In 2024, guests can investigate these common spaces, finding out about reasonable cultivating rehearses and drawing in with neighborhood producers.

Zero-Squander Drives:

Christchurch's obligation to maintainability stretches out to local area drives advancing zero-squander rehearses. Ranchers' business sectors and eco-cognizant occasions grandstand the city's commitment to lessening natural effects.

Culinary Gardens and Homestead to-Table Eating:

Neighborhood Produce and Culinary Greatness:

Christchurch's culinary scene mirrors the city's association with nature. In 2024, ranch-to-table eating encounters permit guests to enjoy dishes produced using privately obtained produce, supplemented by spices and consumable blossoms from eatery gardens.

Botanic Cooking:

A few diners in Christchurch integrate botanic subjects into their food, making dishes enlivened by the different vegetation tracked down in the Botanic Nurseries. These culinary manifestations give an extraordinary and scrumptious method for interfacing with nature.

Dunedin: Scottish Heritage in the South

Settled on the southeastern bank of New Zealand's South Island, Dunedin remains a city that gladly embraces its Scottish legacy, mixing it flawlessly with the normal excellence and social wealth of the locale. In 2024, Dunedin keeps on dazzling guests with its notable design, dynamic expressions scene, and warm Kiwi welcome, making an exceptional embroidery of Scottish impact in the core of the South Island.

Verifiable Roots and Scottish Impact:

Settlement and Engineering:

Laid out by Scottish trailblazers during the nineteenth hundred years, Dunedin holds quite a bit of its legacy as Victorian and Edwardian engineering. The city's memorable structures, for example, the Dunedin Rail Route Station and Larnach Palace, feature the persevering impact of Scottish plan and craftsmanship.

Scottish Road Names:

A stroll through Dunedin uncovers a sign of approval for its Scottish starting points in the road names and spot references. Roads like George Road and Sovereigns Road give recognition to Scottish sovereignty, giving an unmistakable connection to the city's establishing legacy.

Social Tourist spots:

First Church of Otago:

Remaining as a famous image of Dunedin's Scottish legacy, the Main Church of Otago is a hitting Presbyterian church with a Gothic plan. Its transcending tower overwhelms the horizon, and the inside highlights stained glass windows portraying scenes from Scottish history.

Toitū Otago Pilgrims Gallery:

The Toitū Otago Pilgrims Gallery offers a far-reaching venture into Dunedin's past, displaying the narratives of its Scottish pioneers. Displays incorporate antiques, photos, and accounts that feature the difficulties and wins of the people who molded the city.

Widespread developments and Celebrations:

Dunedin Good Country Games:

The yearly Dunedin Good Country Games observe Scottish culture with customary occasions, for example, caber throwing, line and drum exhibitions, and High country moving. A dynamic and exuberant event unites local people and guests with a sense of fellowship.

Edinburgh of the South:

Dunedin's moniker as the "Edinburgh of the South" addresses its Scottish legacy. The city's various stops and gardens, including the Dunedin Botanic Nursery, add to its standing as a city suggestive of the Scottish capital.

Normal Excellence:

Otago Promontory:

Simply a short drive from the downtown area, the Otago Promontory offers a stunning waterfront view and an opportunity to detect natural life like seals, ocean lions, and different seabirds. The promontory's rough scenes give a distinct yet lovely differentiation to Dunedin's metropolitan climate.

Baldwin Road:

Perceived as the world's steepest private road, Baldwin Road adds a particular appeal to Dunedin. The yearly Jaffa Race, where a great many chocolate confections are moved down the precarious incline, is a remarkable and engaging occasion that draws in local people and guests the same.

Nelson and its Artistic Flourish

Nelson settled at the highest point of the South Island, remains a lively center of imaginative articulation, encompassed by pleasant scenes and washed in a sun-doused environment. In 2024, this beguiling city keeps on flourishing as a shelter for imagination, drawing craftsmen, craftsmen, and devotees from around the world. Investigate the imaginative prosperity that characterizes Nelson and make it an interesting jewel on New Zealand's South Island.

Daylight City:

Nelson is warmly known as the "Daylight City" because of its advantageous environment. The bountiful daylight improves the locale's normal magnificence as well as fills in as a steady wellspring of motivation for the imaginative local area. In 2024, Nelson's radiant attitude keeps on making an enticing air for specialists and guests the same.

Elite Workmanship Displays:

Nelson brags a noteworthy exhibit of craftsmanship displays displaying both conventional and contemporary works. The Suter Workmanship Exhibition, in the core of the city, houses a different assortment, including pieces by prestigious New Zealand craftsmen. In 2024, new presentations and intelligent shows further advance the social experience for guests.

Imaginative Territories:

The roads of Nelson are enhanced with public workmanship establishments, wall paintings, and models, making a vivid encounter for those walking around the city. Idiosyncratic back streets and secret corners shock guests with startling imaginative pearls. In 2024, Nelson's obligation to metropolitan beautification guarantees that the cityscape stays a material for imaginative articulation.

Make Breweries and Distinctive Restaurants:

Nelson's imaginative soul reaches out to its culinary scene, creating breweries and distinctive restaurants dissipated all through the city. Nearby brewers team up with craftsmen to make novel marks, changing lager bottles into masterpieces. In 2024, the combination of craftsmanship and gastronomy arrives at new levels, offering guests a great tactile encounter.

Nelson Expressions Celebration:

The Nelson Expressions Celebration, held every year, features a unique mix of visual expressions, music, theater, and writing. In 2024, the celebration has extended to incorporate worldwide joint efforts, encouraging social trade and carrying a worldwide viewpoint to the neighborhood's creative local area.

Imaginative Studios and Studios:

Nelson's imaginative local area is known for its inviting nature, and numerous specialists open their studios to the general population. In 2024, imaginative studios and intuitive meetings furnish guests with the chance to connect straightforwardly with craftsmen, acquiring experiences into their cycles and motivations.

Abel Tasman Public Park: Motivation in Nature:

Simply a short drive from Nelson lies the dazzling Abel Tasman Public Park, a shelter for open-air lovers and specialists the same. The recreation area's brilliant sea shores, turquoise waters, and lavish woodlands have roused endless painters, picture-takers, and essayists. In 2024, eco-accommodating drives guarantee the conservation of this normal magnum opus.

CHAPTER FOUR

Adrenaline Rush: South Island Adventures

Bungee Jumping and Skydiving Hotspots

New Zealand's South Island is famous for its stunning scenes and adrenaline-siphoning experience exercises. In 2024, daredevils from around the globe run to the island's different landscapes to encounter a definitive surge of bungee bouncing and skydiving. From transcending precipices to immaculate shores, the South Island offers a variety of areas of interest that guarantee remarkable aeronautical undertakings.

Queenstown: The Experience Capital of the World
Settled on the shores of Lake Wakatipu, Queenstown is an unmatched center for thrill seekers. In 2024, it keeps on setting its standing as the Experience Capital of the

World, offering both bungee hopping and skydiving encounters that exploit the shocking elevated view.

a. Nevis Bungy: Opposing Gravity

The Nevis Bungy, one of the greatest on the planet, entices daredevils to jump from a suspended unit 134 meters over the Nevis Stream. The drop gives an unrivaled rush as jumpers plunge towards the tough ravine beneath, with the Southern Alps shaping an emotional scenery.

b. Nzone Skydive: Rising above Remarkables

For those hoping to join the adventure of fast drop with spectacular all-encompassing perspectives, Nzone Skydive offers a couple of get around the Remarkables mountain range. Members experience an adrenaline-charged drop before the parachute opens, permitting them to absorb the astounding scenes of Queenstown and Lake Wakatipu.

Taupo: New Levels Over an Old Caldera

In the core of the North Island, Taupo sits on the Taupo Volcanic Zone, offering a one-of-a-kind setting for experienced fans. While not on the South Island, Taupo is a must-specify for its wonderful skydiving encounters that draw adrenaline searchers from all edges of New Zealand and then some.

a. Taupo Bungy: Rushes Over the Waikato Waterway

The Taupo Bungy welcomes jumpers to go out on a limb from a stage suspended over the strong Waikato Stream. The dazzling scenery of New Zealand's biggest lake and the snow-covered pinnacles of Tongariro Public Park add a layer of energy to this elating experience.

b. Skydive Taupo: Jump Into the Incomparable Lake Taupo Perspectives

Skydive Taupo offers a couple of skydiving experience that features the famous Extraordinary Lake Taupo. Jumpers drop from up to 15,000 feet, appreciating continuous perspectives on the lake, Tongariro Public Park, and the Focal North Island.

Fox Glacial mass: An Ice sheet Skydive Like No Other

For an extraordinary skydiving experience, the Fox Icy mass on the South Island's West Coast stands apart as an entrancing scenery. Skydivers here partake in an unrivaled perspective on the tremendous Southern Alps and the tough West Coast territory.

a. Skydive Fox Ice sheet: Frigid Drop

Skydive Fox Icy Mass takes the experience higher than ever with hops from up to 16,000 feet. The drop over the striking scene, with looks at the namesake icy mass and the Tasman Ocean, makes this a remarkable skydiving area of interest.

Water Adventures: Kayaking, Rafting, and More

New Zealand's South Island is a shelter for water devotees, offering an elating cluster of sea-going encounters against the scenery of dazzling scenes. In 2024, the water undertakings of kayaking, boating, and more keep spellbinding daredevils and nature sweethearts the same. From the unblemished streams and cold lakes to the rough shorelines, we should investigate the different water exercises that make the South Island a chief objective for oceanic ventures.

Kayaking in Milford Sound: Rowing Heaven
Fiordland Magnificence: Milford Sound, a UNESCO World Legacy site, is a kayaker's heaven, encompassed by transcending tops, flowing cascades, and lavish rainforests. In 2024, directed kayak visits permit globe-trotters to paddle near seals, and dolphins, and even catch a brief look at the subtle Fiordland peaked penguin.

Short-term Undertakings: For the more brave, multi-day kayak endeavors give a vivid encounter, permitting members to camp along the shores of Milford Sound and associate with the unblemished wild.

Queenstown: The Experience Capital for Boating Fans

Kawarau Stream Rushes: Queenstown, famous as the experience capital of New Zealand, flaunts exciting boating encounters on the Kawarau Waterway. The Shotover and Kawarau Streams offer a scope of rapids, making it reasonable for the two fledglings and prepared rafters.

Helicopter and Boating Combo: In 2024, imaginative visit administrators are offering helicopter-got to boating undertakings, joining the adventure of a flying excursion with the energy of exploring the rapids.

Frigid Kayaking on Tasman Lake: Ice Shelves and High Greatness

Icy mass Took care of Wonder: Tasman Lake, framed by the Tasman Ice sheet, gives an extraordinary kayaking experience encompassed by drifting chunks of ice. In 2024, directed visits take paddlers through the dreamlike scene of turquoise waters, antiquated ice sheets, and the transcending pinnacles of the Southern Alps.

Environment Cognizant Experiences: With a developing accentuation on maintainable the travel industry, icy kayaking administrators are carrying out eco-accommodating practices to limit the effect on this delicate elevated biological system.

Ocean Kayaking in Abel Tasman Public Park: Brilliant Sea Shores and Secret Bays

Waterfront Heaven: Abel Tasman Public Park is a beachfront diamond, offering ocean kayaking open doors along its brilliant sea shores and disconnected inlets. In 2024, ocean kayaking journeys give a close investigation of marine life, including seals, dolphins, and a heap of bird animal varieties.

Setting up camp and Kayaking Breaks: Travelers can leave on multi-day ventures, setting up camp along the shore and awakening to the sound of waves, making a vivid association with nature.

Versatile Water Sports: Inclusivity and Openness

Open Undertakings: In 2024, the South Island's water experience scene will become more comprehensive, with versatile kayaking and boating programs taking special care of people with different capacities. These drives guarantee that everybody, paying little mind to actual capacity, can participate in the adventure of water-based exercises.

Skiing and Snowboarding in the Southern Alps

New Zealand's South Island is a colder time of year wonderland, home to the great Southern Alps and offering lovers a jungle gym for skiing and snowboarding undertakings. As you gear up for a thrilling winter season in 2024, the Southern Alps coax with unblemished slants, dazzling scenes, and plenty of exercises for snow sports fans.

Picking Your Objective:

The Southern Alps brag a few top-notch ski resorts, each with its remarkable appeal. Queenstown, Wanaka, and Methven are among the top objections, offering a different scope of slants reasonable for all expertise levels.

Consider factors like landscape, conveniences, and openness while picking your objective, guaranteeing it lines up with your inclinations and expertise level.

The Ski Resorts:

Queenstown:

Eminent as the experience capital, Queenstown offers admittance to two significant ski fields - Coronet

Pinnacle and The Remarkables. Both give a blend of prepared trails and testing off-piste runs.

Wanaka:

Home to Cardrona Snow-capped Hotel and High Pitch Cone, Wanaka grandstands stunning elevated views. Cardrona is renowned for its territory park, while High Pitch Cone offers far-reaching slants for moderate and high-level skiers.

Methven:

Mount Hutt in Methven is known for its solid snow conditions and changed territory. Taking special care of all ability levels, it's a superb decision for families and experienced snow sports lovers the same.

Territory and Conditions:

The Southern Alps offer a different scope of territory, from delicate slants for novices to testing backwoods courses for specialists.

Watch out for atmospheric conditions and torrential slide alerts, particularly if wandering into off-piste regions. Neighborhood ski watch and data focuses give modern data to guarantee a protected and pleasant experience.

Winter Occasions:

Plan your visit to harmonize with significant winter occasions and celebrations. The Southern Half of the globe's colder time of year takes into account novel chances to observe worldwide contests, energetic festivals, and comprehensive developments that add to the general insight.

Après-Ski Exercises:

Past the slants, the Southern Alps locale offers a large group of après-ski exercises. Investigate the beguiling towns, enjoy neighborhood cooking, and loosen up in hot pools to loosen up following a completely exhilarating day on the mountains.

Hardware Rental and Illustrations:

Whether you're an old pro or a novice, the Southern Alps have first-class hardware rental offices and experienced teachers to take care of all expertise levels.

Put resources into quality stuff and exploit illustrations to upgrade your abilities and take advantage of your experience on the slants.

Ecological Stewardship:

Regard the regular excellence of the Southern Alps by sticking to Leave No Follow standards. Be aware of waste, follow assigned trails, and back up eco-accommodating drives inside the ski resorts.

Wildlife Encounters

Kaikoura: Whale Watching Hub

In 2024, Kaikoura keeps on supreme as a definitive whale-watching objective on New Zealand's South Island, offering an unmatched marine scene that catches the hearts of nature devotees around the world. Settled between the Pacific Sea and the transcending Kaikoura Reaches, this beachfront pearl is praised for its rich marine biodiversity and the chance to observe magnificent marine well-evolved creatures right at home. Go along with us as we set out on an excursion to investigate Kaikoura, the unparalleled whale-watching center of the South Island.

Marine Wonders: Whales of Kaikoura:
Sperm Whales:
Kaikoura is eminent for its all-year inhabitant populace of sperm whales — the biggest-toothed whales on earth. In 2024, guests can observe these heavenly animals nimbly surfacing and making a plunge into the profound waters simply seaward.

Orca, Humpback, from there, the sky is the limit:
Past sperm whales, Kaikoura's marine jungle gym draws in a different exhibit of marine life, including orcas,

humpback whales, and lively dolphins. The supplement-rich waters give a plentiful gala to these marine monsters, making a flourishing environment.

Whale Watching Visits:
Kaikoura Whale Watch Visits:
Kaikoura's particular whale watching visits, accessible in 2024, offer an exhilarating and open door to notice whales very close. Educated guides give bits of knowledge into the way of behaving and science of the marine well-evolved creatures, improving the general insight.

Extraordinary Vantage Focuses:
Boats furnished with cutting-edge hydrophones permit travelers to pay attention to the entrancing submerged hints of whales. Moreover, picturesque flights give a stunning flying point of view, displaying the scale and magnificence of these marine wonders.

Dolphin Experiences:

Dim Dolphins:

Kaikoura's waters are additionally home to energetic shadowy dolphins. In 2024, guests can participate in dolphin experiences, where these enthusiastic and gymnastic dolphins frequently join boats, displaying their wonderful dexterity and energy for human organization.

Swimming with Dolphins:

For the more gutsy, swimming with dolphins is an extraordinary encounter. Directed visits give a protected and deferential method for connecting with these keen animals right at home.

Seabird Scene:

Gooney bird Experiences:

Kaikoura's beachfront area makes a safe house for seabirds, including the grand gooney bird. Specific visits offer birdwatchers and nature fans the chance to notice these noteworthy birds taking off over the waves.

Pelagic Birdlife:

Kaikoura's nearness to the mainland rack draws in a wide assortment of pelagic bird species, making it a birdwatcher's heaven. Optics close by, guests can recognize shearwaters, petrels, and gooney birds against the background of the vast sea.

Kaikoura Promontory Walkway: Seaside Excellence and Marine Perspectives:

Grand Seaside Walk:

The Kaikoura Promontory Walkway, in 2024, offers a vivid encounter mixing seaside excellence and marine perspectives. Explorers can appreciate dazzling scenes of the Pacific Sea, the Toward the Ocean Kaikoura Reach, and, with karma, spot marine life from the raised vantage focus.

Fur Seal States:

The walkway additionally prompts settlements of New Zealand fur seals. Noticing these fun-loving and inquisitive animals right at home adds to the charm of the seaside journey.

Culinary Joys: Fish Capital:

New Fish:

Kaikoura's status as the fish capital of New Zealand is reflected in its culinary contributions. In 2024, guests can enjoy newly got fish, including crawfish, mussels, and an assortment of fish, making a gastronomic encounter that supplements the seaside feel.

Shoreline Feasting:

Eateries along the waterfront offer the ideal setting for partaking in a fish feast while taking in all-encompassing perspectives on the sea. Kaikoura's fish is praised for its newness and remarkable flavors.

Protection and Supportability:

Eco-Accommodating Practices:

Kaikoura puts serious areas of strength in marine preservation and reasonable the travel industry. Whale-watching administrators comply with severe rules to limit the unsettling influence on marine life, guaranteeing a mindful and eco-accommodating experience for guests.

Local area Commitment:

The neighborhood local area effectively takes part in marine preservation endeavors. Instructive projects and local area drives add to the mindfulness and assurance of Kaikoura's interesting marine climate.

Penguin Colonies and Seabird Sanctuaries

The South Island of New Zealand is a gold mine for bird devotees and nature sweethearts the same, bragging exhibit penguin settlements and seabird safe-havens. In

2024, these seaside shelters keep on filling in as crucial protection destinations, giving a home to a different scope of seabird species. From the magnetic penguins to the grand gooney birds, the South Island's seaside scenes exhibit the flourishing avian life that graces the shores of this staggering locale.

Penguin Provinces:

Yellow-peered toward Penguins (Hoiho):

One of the most uncommon and most notable penguins, the yellow-peered toward penguins, or Hoiho, track down shelter in a few areas across the South Island. Oamaru and the Otago Promontory are especially known for their preservation endeavors, giving open doors to guests to notice these extraordinary birds right at home.

Minimal Blue Penguins (Kororā):

The littlest of all penguin species, the little blue penguins, or Kororā, make states along the South Island's shore. Spots like Akaroa and the Marlborough

Sounds offer directed visits to observe the beguiling daily motorcade of these slight birds getting back from the ocean to their homes.

Fiordland Peaked Penguins (Tawaki):

Remote and tricky, the Fiordland Peaked Penguins, or Tawaki, breed in the coves of the South Island. The rough and immaculate scenes of Fiordland Public Park give a one-of-a-kind setting to notice these penguins, frequently settling in confined spots from human movement.

Seabird Asylums:

Kaikoura Landmass:

The Kaikoura Landmass, eminent for its rich marine life, is likewise home to an assortment of seabird animal types. Gooney birds, petrels, and shearwaters can be spotted rising above the seaside bluffs, making a hypnotizing exhibition for birdwatchers and natural life fans.

Dunedin's Taiaroa Head:

Taiaroa Head on the Otago Promontory is home to the main central area rearing settlement of Illustrious Gooney birds on the planet. Directed visits offer a close encounter to observe these superb birds in their settling climate, exhibiting their noteworthy wingspan and effortless flight.

Whale Watch at Kaikoura:

While principally known for whale watching, Kaikoura likewise has a flourishing populace of seabirds. Guests on whale watching visits are frequently treated to seeing gooney birds, shearwaters, and different seabirds effortlessly exploring the sea flows.

Preservation and Exploration:

The South Island's penguin states and seabird safe havens assume an urgent part in preservation endeavors. Different associations team up to safeguard settling locales, screen populaces, and lead examinations to all the more likely grasp the way of behaving and needs of these birds. Visit administrators frequently contribute a part of their returns to help these preservation drives.

Guest Encounters:

Directed Visits and Survey Stages:

Numerous areas offer directed visits and all-around planned survey stages that permit guests to notice seabirds without upsetting their normal ways of behaving. Educated guides give bits of knowledge about the existence of these interesting animals and the protection challenges they face.

Natural life Travels:

Natural life travels in locales like Fiordland and Kaikoura offer a special viewpoint, permitting guests to observe seabirds against the background of stunning waterfront landscapes. The sheer wealth of birdlife here is a demonstration of the flourishing environment.

Conservation Efforts and Eco-Friendly Initiatives

New Zealand's South Island, commended for its unmatched normal magnificence, perfect scenes, and novel biodiversity, is at the very front of worldwide preservation endeavors and supportable practices. In 2024, a large group of creative drives and committed protection programs are molding the island's obligation to safeguard its natural fortunes, guaranteeing that people in the future can keep on wondering about its immaculate quality.

Hunger-Free New Zealand:

At the front of South Island's preservation is the aggressive objective of becoming hunter-free by 2050. Protection associations, neighborhood networks, and the public authority team up to annihilate presented hunters like rodents, stoats, and possums that undermine local bird species. In 2024, creative catching techniques and hereditary advances will be utilized to speed up progress toward this aggressive objective.

Safeguarded Regions and Public Parks:

New Zealand's South Island is home to various public stops and safeguarded regions, protecting its assorted biological systems. In 2024, these districts benefit from expanded financing and key protection plans pointed toward saving native verdure. Drives likewise center around reestablishing territories and once again introducing imperiled species to their indigenous habitats.

Reasonable travel industry Practices:

Perceiving the effect of the travel industry on delicate biological systems, South Island embraces reasonable travel industry rehearses. In 2024, eco-accommodating facilities, squander decrease measures, and dependable visit administrators guarantee that guests can investigate the island's marvels without undermining its regular honesty. Training programs bring issues to light about limiting the natural impression of the travel industry.

Eco-Accommodating Transportation:

South Island is focused on decreasing fossil fuel byproducts, with drives advancing eco-accommodating transportation. In 2024, electric vehicle framework, bicycle sharing projects, and further developed public transportation choices add to a more supportable travel insight, empowering the two local people and guests to investigate the island with negligible ecological effect.

Marine Preservation Drives:

The waters encompassing South Island are wealthy in marine life, and preservation endeavors stretch out to safeguard its waterfront environments. In 2024, marine stores are extended, fishing guidelines are fortified, and local area-driven drives advance economical fishing rehearses. Instructive projects feature the significance of safeguarding marine biodiversity.

Local area Drove Preservation Undertakings:

Nearby people groups effectively take part in protection projects, encouraging a feeling of stewardship and association with the land. In 2024, the local area drove drives centered around establishing local trees, reestablishing wetlands, and making untamed life halls. These tasks upgrade biodiversity as well as fortify the connection between individuals and their current circumstances.

Native Information and Maori Protection Practices:

South Island perceives the priceless commitment of native information in protection. In 2024, Maori protection rehearses, established in a profound comprehension of the land, assume a fundamental part in forming economic administration methodologies. Conventional methodologies are coordinated with present-day preservation science to make comprehensive and successful protection arrangements.

CHAPTER FIVE

Culinary Delights

Kiwi Cuisine: A Gastronomic Journey

Leaving on a culinary experience through New Zealand's South Island in 2024 is a tactile joy, as the district flaunts a dynamic food scene that mirrors its different scenes and social impacts. From new fish along the shore to good sheep dishes in the elevated locales, the Kiwi food of the South Island is a heavenly excursion of flavors and development.

Kaikoura: Fish Spectacle by the Pacific Sea
Settled along the tough shoreline of the South Island, Kaikoura is a fish darling's heaven, offering a blowout of sea treasures obtained from the flawless waters of the Pacific. In 2024, the town's fish markets and diners

proceed to grandstand the best of New Zealand's amphibian abundance.

a. Crawfish (Kaikoura Rock Lobster): Maritime Extravagance

Kaikoura is famous for its delicious crawfish, otherwise called Kaikoura rock lobster. Privately got and skillfully ready, this delicacy is frequently served barbecued with garlic margarine, permitting the normal pleasantness of the crawfish to sparkle. Guests can relish this maritime extravagance at waterfront cafés with all-encompassing perspectives on the Pacific Sea.

b. Green-Lipped Mussels: Flavors from the Profundities

The green-lipped mussels collected from the beachfront waters close to Kaikoura are another culinary feature. These full and delightful mollusks are in many cases ready in various ways, from exemplary steaming in white wine and garlic to imaginative dishes that grandstand the variety of New Zealand's fish.

Canterbury Fields: Sheep, Wine, and Rural Greatness

Making a beeline for the Canterbury Fields, the scene changes into lavish farmland, making way for a festival of peaceful pleasures. In 2024, Canterbury will keep on being a gastronomic center point, with its rich farming produce and grant-winning wineries.

a. Canterbury Sheep: A Culinary Symbol

Canterbury sheep is a staple of Kiwi cooking, commended for its delicacy and special flavor profile. Neighborhood gourmet experts make imaginative dishes, from slow-cooked legs of lamb to appetizing sheep pies, permitting guests to relish the pith of New Zealand's peaceful scenes.

b. Waipara Valley Wines: Grape plantation Polish

The nearby Waipara Valley is a wine darling's shelter, creating top-notch Pinot Noirs, Rieslings, and Sauvignon Blancs. Wineries offer tastings against the setting of the

Southern Alps, giving an ideal supplement to the locale's luscious cooking.

Focal Otago: Plantations, Grape Plantations, and Pinot Noir Flawlessness

Wandering further south, Focal Otago's assorted scenes yield a wealth of natural products, vegetables, and, most prominently, outstanding Pinot Noir wines. The locale's plantations and grape plantations add to a culinary encounter that typifies the embodiment of New Zealand's South Island.

a. Stone Organic product Joys: Plantations of Cromwell

Focal Otago is popular for its stone natural product plantations, especially apricots, cherries, and peaches. Guests can enjoy new natural products directly from the plantations or appreciate debauched pastries including these occasional diamonds.

b. Pinot Noir Pairings: Wine sampling in Gibbston Valley

Gibbston Valley, known as the "Valley of the Plants," is a chief wine-creating locale, particularly famous for its Pinot Noir. Wineries in Gibbston Valley offer tastings that grandstand the nuanced kinds of this outstanding wine impeccably matched with nearby cheeses and distinctive charges.

Wineries and Vineyard Tours

New Zealand's South Island, famous for its stunning scenes, is likewise a prospering center point for wine devotees looking to investigate the different and thriving wine locales. In 2024, the wineries and grape plantation voyages through the South Island keep on captivating guests with their top-notch wines, beautiful settings, and a promise to reasonable viticulture. We should open up the tale of New Zealand's South Island, where each taste is an excursion through the terroir and custom.

Marlborough: Sauvignon Blanc Heaven

Sauvignon Blanc Perfect world: Marlborough remains as a worldwide symbol for Sauvignon Blanc, delivering a portion of the world's most commended articulations of this varietal. In 2024, grape plantation visits in Marlborough offer a vivid encounter, from walking around plant-covered slopes to tasting the district's unique fresh and fragrant wines.

Wine and Workmanship Combination: Numerous Marlborough wineries have embraced the collaboration among wine and craftsmanship, including figures and establishments that improve the stylish delight of the wine sampling experience.

Focal Otago: Pinot Noir Wonderland

Stunning Scenes: Focal Otago, known for its sensational snow-capped view, is a sanctuary for Pinot Noir lovers. Grape plantation visits in this district grandstand the difficult yet compensating terroir, as well as the careful craftsmanship behind each container of Pinot Noir.

Cavern and Basement Encounters: In 2024, a few wineries in Focal Otago offer special basement encounters, permitting guests to investigate underground caverns where wines improve with age. These barometrical settings add a layer of interest to the tasting venture.

Canterbury: Cool Environment Class

Waipara Valley Pearls: Canterbury's Waipara Valley has earned respect for its cool-environment wines, especially Riesling and Pinot Gris. In 2024, grape plantation visits in this district give a chance to relish the rich and fragrant articulations of these varietals while appreciating all-encompassing perspectives on the Southern Alps.

Gastronomic Encounters: Some Canterbury wineries have arranged gastronomic encounters, matching their wines with neighborhood rarities. These culinary experiences lift the tasting meeting, making an orchestra of flavors on the sense of taste.

Nelson: Aesthetic Wines and Natural Pleasures

Imaginative Plants: Nelson, frequently alluded to as the "Inventive Capital," mixes creative energy into its winemaking. Guests in 2024 can investigate wineries where workmanship and wine meet, with marks highlighting exceptional plans and tasting rooms serving as exhibitions.

Natural and Biodynamic Practices: Nelson has embraced natural and biodynamic viticulture, for certain wineries displaying their obligation to maintainability. Grape plantation visits frequently incorporate experiences into these works, cultivating an appreciation for earth-cognizant wine creation.

Wairarapa: Store Greatness

Martinborough Appeal: Wairarapa's Martinborough locale is a store wine objective, praised for its exceptional Pinot Noir and Chardonnay. In 2024, grape plantation visits in Martinborough give a private encounter, permitting guests to meet winemakers, walk around notable grape plantations, and appreciate restricted version discharges.

Cycling and Wine Trails: To improve the tasting experience, a few wineries in Wairarapa offer cycling and wine trail encounters, permitting devotees to pedal through beautiful scenes and stop for tastings at different homes.

Local Markets and Food Festivals

New Zealand's South Island is a gastronomic sanctuary, where neighborhood markets and food celebrations grandstand the district's different flavors, high-quality items, and culinary development. In 2024, submerge yourself in the energetic food culture of the South Island, where new produce, connoisseur delights, and social encounters are anticipated every step of the way.

Christchurch Ranchers' Market:

Settled in the core of Christchurch, the ranchers' market is a cornucopia of privately obtained produce, high-quality merchandise, and flavorful treats. From natural products of the soil to craftsman cheeses and newly heated merchandise, the market offers a banquet for the faculties.

Draw in with nearby ranchers and makers, finding out about feasible practices and the tales behind the items. The market's air is vivacious, with unrecorded music and a feeling of the local area adding to the general insight.

Nelson Market:

Known for its refined and easygoing energy, the Nelson Market is a gold mine of handmade products, global cooking, and live diversion. Peruse slows down exhibiting one-of-a-kind workmanship, gems, and dress before enjoying worldwide flavors from the different food merchants.

Queenstown Night Market:

As the sun sets over Queenstown, the Night Market shows some signs of life, offering a culinary experience under the stars. Test various global cooking styles, from Japanese road food to Mediterranean pleasures, all while partaking in the background of Lake Wakatipu and the Remarkables mountain range.

Wanaka Food and Wine Celebration:

The Wanaka Food and Wine Celebration is a feature on the South Island's culinary schedule. Set against the staggering background of Lake Wanaka, this occasion unites nearby wineries, breweries, and diners for a day of tastings and live diversion. Participants can appreciate grant-winning wines, specialty lagers, and connoisseur dishes made by capable culinary experts.

Marlborough Wine and Food Celebration:

Famous as one of New Zealand's chief wine occasions, the Marlborough Wine and Food Celebration is a festival of the district's top-notch wines and delightful cooking.

Set in the pleasant Brancott Grape plantation, the celebration highlights tastings, unrecorded music, and the opportunity to meet the winemakers behind the eminent Marlborough Sauvignon Blanc.

Kaikoura Seafest:

Fish darlings cheer at the Kaikoura Seafest, a celebration devoted to the locale's plentiful marine contributions. From crawfish to paua, the occasion grandstands Kaikoura's rich fish culture with cooking exhibits, tastings, and a vivacious climate by the sea.

Neighborhood Flavors and Social Encounters:

Past the business sectors and celebrations, investigate nearby diners and eateries to appreciate South Island's strengths. Enjoy the popular Fergburger in Queenstown, test Feign shellfish, and attempt customary Maori hangi, a strategy for cooking utilizing warmed rocks covered in the ground.

Accommodations: From Luxury Retreats to Charming B&Bs

Unique Stays: Glamping and Wilderness Lodges

In 2024, the South Island of New Zealand coaxes voyagers to encounter the encapsulation of extravagance in the lap of nature. Embracing the way of thinking of practical and vivid travel, the district offers one-of-a-kind stays that rethink the conventional idea of convenience. From breathtaking setting up camp (glamping) destinations that mix solace with nature to wild hotels settled in unblemished scenes, the South Island welcomes guests to enjoy unmatched encounters. Go along with us on an excursion to investigate the unmistakable appeal of glamping and wild hotels, where extravagance meets nature as one.

Eco-Accommodating Glamping Retreats:

Aro Ha Wellbeing Retreat:

Aro Ha, situated close to Queenstown, is an incredibly famous health retreat that flawlessly joins extravagance with supportability. In 2024, visitors can remain in eco-accommodating glamping cases settled in the Southern Alps. These moderate yet lavish cases offer all-encompassing perspectives on Lake Wakatipu and the encompassing mountains.

Maintainability Concentration:

Aro Ha focuses on eco-accommodating works on, integrating sun oriented energy, water reaping, and natural cultivating. The glamping experience here permits visitors to interface with nature while partaking in the solaces of a well-being-centered retreat.

Isolated Glamping at Minaret Station:

Minaret Station:

For those looking for disconnection in the core of the Southern Alps, Minaret Station offers a selective glamping experience available exclusively by helicopter. Each sumptuous tent, encompassed by snow-covered tops and elevated glades, gives a confidential retreat in quite possibly one of the most far-off areas in New Zealand.

Helicopter Access:

In 2024, visitors can show up at Minaret Station using a beautiful helicopter ride, establishing the vibe for a restrictive and vivid experience. The glamping tents are furnished with current conveniences, guaranteeing an agreeable and extravagant stay.

Wild Cabins Amid Fiordland's Highness:

Fiordland Cabin:

Settled on a slope sitting above Lake Te Anau and encompassed by Fiordland Public Park, Fiordland Cabin is a wild retreat that catches the substance of the South Island's untamed excellence. In 2024, visitors can remain in roomy and exquisitely designated rooms, each offering all-encompassing perspectives on the lake and mountains.

Nature Drenching:

Fiordland Cabin gives a door to Fiordland's famous scenes. Visitors can investigate close-by strolling tracks, journey on Milford Sound, and return to the cabin for connoisseur eating and unwinding in a quiet elevated setting.

Extravagance Tents at Kahu Kayaks:

Kahu Kayaks Glamping:

Situated in Marahau, the doorway to Abel Tasman Public Park, Kahu Kayaks offers a remarkable glamping experience in extravagant safari tents. In 2024, visitors can partake in the hints of the close by sea and local birds while remaining in wonderfully outfitted tents with private decks.

Kayaking Experiences:

Kahu Kayaks has some expertise in directed kayaking undertakings, permitting visitors to investigate the perfect waters of Abel Tasman. The glamping experience supplements the open-air exercises, giving an agreeable and beautiful retreat following a day of investigation.

Treehouse Getaways at Hapuku Hotel:

Hapuku Cabin and Tree Houses:

Settled between Kaikoura's mountains and the Pacific Sea, Hapuku Cabin offers a charming departure with its extravagant treehouse facilities. In 2024, visitors can remain in raised treehouses, encompassed by local kanuka trees, with staggering perspectives on the Kaikoura mountains and the coast.

Culinary Greatness:

Hapuku Cabin flaunts an eminent café that underlines privately obtained and occasional fixings. Visitors can enjoy connoisseur feasts while submerged in the peacefulness of the encompassing normal excellence.

Elevated Extravagance at Cover Straight:

Cover Sound Cabin:

Set against the background of the Southern Alps and Lake Wakatipu, Cover Straight Cabin close to Glenorchy offers a sumptuous snow-capped retreat. In 2024, visitors can encounter the embodiment of complexity in confidential chalets with dazzling perspectives, rich goods, and customized administration.

Experience and Unwinding:

Cover Narrows Hotel gives admittance to a scope of outside exercises, from heli-skiing to climbing. Following a day of experience, visitors can loosen up in the cabin's spa, hot tub, or by the thundering fire in the Incomparable Room.

Momentous Glamping at Camp Glenorchy:

Camp Glenorchy:

Frequently alluded to as New Zealand's most memorable net-positive eco-stop, Camp Glenorchy sets another norm for practical and upscale convenience. In 2024, visitors can encounter glamping in mindfully planned eco-lodges encompassed by the dazzling scenes of Glenorchy.

Net-Positive Eco-Hotel:

Camp Glenorchy is focused on natural supportability, highlighting energy-proficient plans, squander decreases, and regenerative practices. The glamping experience here permits visitors to associate with nature while limiting their biological impression.

Eco-Friendly Accommodations

In 2024, as natural cognizance keeps on molding travel inclinations, New Zealand's South Island becomes the overwhelming focus as a shelter for eco-accommodating facilities. From the rough scenes of Fiordland to the seaside appeal of Kaikoura, a developing number of lodgings are embracing feasible works, furnishing guests with the chance to encounter the South Island's normal marvels while limiting their biological impression.

Eco-Hotels in Fiordland Public Park:
Settled inside the stunning scenes of Fiordland, eco-lodges epitomize maintainability in both plan and activity. These lodgings frequently consolidate sustainable power sources, eco-accommodating development materials, and practices that limit their effect on the fragile biological systems of the district. Guests can drench themselves in nature without settling for less on ecological obligation.

Off-the-Network Retreats in Wanaka:

Wanaka, encompassed by a high landscape, has off-the-framework withdraws that take care of eco-cognizant explorers looking for a reasonable break. These facilities use sun-based power, water collecting, and low-influence building procedures to give a peaceful retreat while saving unblemished environmental elements.

Kaikoura's Eco-Accommodating Ocean-side Hotels:

With its rich marine life and waterfront appeal, Kaikoura offers eco-accommodating coastline motels that focus on natural protection. These lodgings frequently execute water-saving drives, squander decrease rehearses, and team up with neighborhood preservation endeavors to safeguard the marine biological systems that make Kaikoura an exceptional objective.

Queenstown's Green Shop Inns:

Queenstown, a center point for experience searchers, highlights green store lodgings focused on maintainability. These facilities consolidate energy-effective advancements, advance waste decrease, and frequently take part in local area-based drives to help the district's natural versatility.

Economical Practices:

Environmentally friendly power Sources:

Numerous eco-accommodating facilities bridle the force of environmentally friendly power, like sunlight-based chargers and wind turbines, to limit their dependence on ordinary energy sources. This decreases their carbon impression as well as features a guarantee to perfect, maintainable practices.

Water Preservation Drives:

Water is a valuable asset, particularly in districts like the South Island. Eco-accommodating facilities carry out water-saving measures, including productive water system frameworks, water collecting, and low-stream apparatuses, to guarantee mindful water utilization without compromising visitor solace.

Squander Decrease and Reusing Projects:

Eco-accommodating lodgings focus on squandering decrease by executing thorough reusing programs, fertilizing the soil, and limiting single-use plastics. Visitors are frequently urged to partake in these drives, cultivating a feeling of ecological obligation.

Nearby and Supportable Obtaining:

Supporting nearby networks and diminishing the carbon impression of food and conveniences is a typical practice in eco-accommodating facilities. Numerous foundations source their items locally, guaranteeing an association with the district's rural contributions while advancing manageability in the store network.

Visitor Instruction and Commitment:

Eco-accommodating facilities in the South Island effectively connect with visitors in natural mindfulness. Enlightening materials, directed eco-visits, and on-location drives teach guests about the delicate biological systems they are investigating and empower mindful travel rehearses.

Hidden Gems and Boutique Hotels

In the core of New Zealand's South Island lies an embroidery of unlikely treasures and shop lodgings, each offering a special mix of extravagance, customized administration, and a personal association with the stunning scenes that encompass them. In 2024, knowing voyagers looking for a particular encounter track down comfort in the cautiously organized appeal of these shop facilities, revealing the genuine substance of South Island's cordiality.

The Marlborough Sounds Retreat: Serenity Reclassified:

Settled in the separated excellence of the Marlborough Sounds, this shop retreat offers a break into nature's hug. Confidential manors, each with all-encompassing perspectives on the Sounds, give a quiet setting. In 2024, the retreat presents vivid eco-encounters, permitting visitors to associate with the immaculate marine climate.

Arthur's Pass High Hotel: Wild Tastefulness:

Set against the background of the Southern Alps, the Arthur's Pass High Hotel consistently mixes provincial enchantment with current tastefulness. In 2024, the hotel will present customized directed climbs and stargazing encounters, benefiting from its area inside the Global Dim Sky Save.

Hapuku Treehouses: Treetop Extravagance in Kaikoura:

Concealed amid local Kanuka woods, the Hapuku Treehouses in Kaikoura rethink extravagance and convenience. Each treehouse is a show-stopper, offering unmatched perspectives on the Pacific Sea and the Kaikoura mountain ranges. In 2024, the property upgrades its obligation to supportability with eco-cognizant practices.

The Resurgence: Eco-Luxury Retreat in Abel Tasman:
Encircled by rich local shrubs in the Abel Tasman district, The Resurgence sets the norm for eco-luxury withdraws. In 2024, the hotel grows its natural nurseries, giving ranch-to-table eating encounters. Visitors can likewise take part in protection exercises, adding to the hotel's obligation to save the climate.

Queenstown's Millbrook Resort: Elevated Plushness:
Ignoring the Remarkables mountain range, Millbrook Resort in Queenstown joins high beguile with elite conveniences. The hotel's store bungalows and estates gloat rich insides and confidential outside spaces. In 2024, Millbrook will present select culinary encounters

and well-being retreats to supplement its upscale contributions.

Fiordland Hotel: Lakeside Serenity:

Arranged on the shores of Lake Te Anau, Fiordland Hotel embodies lakeside serenity. Floor-to-roof windows exhibit the greatness of the encompassing Fiordland Public Park. In 2024, the hotel will upgrade its connoisseur encounters, offering visitors the chance to enjoy privately obtained rarities matched with territorial wines.

Akaroa's The French Ranch style home: Ageless Tastefulness:

In the beguiling town of Akaroa, The French Ranch style home is a sanctuary of immortal polish. Independently planned suites, motivated by French commonplace style, give a cozy break. In 2024, the property presents arranged craftsmanship and culinary encounters, praising the combination of French complexity and South Island beguile.

Nelson's Almyra Waterfront Cabin: Ocean side Rapture:
Sitting above Tasman Narrows in Nelson, Almyra Waterfront Cabin offers a peaceful ocean-side retreat. With just a small bunch of suites, this shop's convenience guarantees customized consideration. In 2024, the hotel will improve its beachfront encounters, offering kayaking and paddleboarding undertakings in the flawless waters.

CHAPTER SIX

Making Money While Traveling in New Zealand's South Island (2024)

Remote Work Opportunities

In the consistently advancing scene of work, the ascent of far-off open doors has opened up additional opportunities for people looking to consolidate their adoration for movement with monetary manageability. New Zealand's South Island, with its shocking scenes and dynamic urban communities, gives a special scenery to those hoping to embrace the computerized traveler's way of life. In 2024, various remote work open doors can help people store their movements as well as drench themselves in the excellence and culture of this captivating district.

Outsourcing and Online Stages: Taking advantage of Worldwide Open doors

a. Upwork and Specialist: Exploring the Gig Economy

Stages like Upwork and Consultant associate specialists with clients around the world, offering valuable open doors recorded as a hard copy, visual communication, web improvement, and that's just the beginning. Embrace your abilities and make a profile that features your skill, permitting you to take on projects while investigating the grand miracles of the South Island.

b. Remote Instructing and Coaching: Teach from Anyplace

For those enthusiastically for instruction, stages like VIPKid or Chegg Guides offer chances to educate or coach on the web. Whether you're a confirmed educator or have skills in a particular subject, remote education permits you to keep an adaptable timetable while procuring pay.

Advanced Advertising and Web-based Entertainment The executives: Displaying the South Island

a. Content Creation: Embrace the Visual Allure

If you have a talent for photography, videography, or content creation, influence stages like Instagram, YouTube, or TikTok to feature the excellence of the South Island. Team up with nearby organizations for supported content or use member showcasing to produce pay while investigating and sharing your encounters.

b. Web-based Entertainment The board: Adapt Your Abilities

Organizations needing web-based entertainment presence frequently enlist distant online entertainment supervisors. Use your skill in connecting with content, overseeing plans, and dissecting measurements to help organizations layout and keep areas of strength for a presence.

Remote Counseling and Training: Offer Your Aptitude

a. Business Counseling: Offer Bits of knowledge from A far distance

For experts with industry ability, remote counseling gives a road to share experiences and proposition important exhortation to organizations. Stages like Clarity. fm interface advisors with clients looking for direction, permitting you to give skill while partaking in the South Island's miracles.

b. Life or Profession Training: Motivate and Engage

Assuming that you have training abilities, consider offering distant life or vocation instructing administrations. Stages like Coach. I or Zoom furnish a virtual space to interface with clients, assisting them with accomplishing individual or expert objectives while you investigate the different scenes of the South Island.

Virtual Help and Authoritative Help: Put together from Anyplace

a. Virtual Help: Backing Organizations From a distance

Organizations and business people frequently look for remote helpers for assignments going from email the board to the information section. Stages like Time And so on and Belay associate gifted colleagues with clients, giving a chance to contribute from a distance while going through the South Island.

b. Online Regulatory Administrations: Effective and Remote

Offer explicit regulatory administrations like record, accounting, or undertaking the executives through stages like Fiverr or TaskRabbit. This permits you to offer significant help to organizations while keeping up with the adaptability to investigate your environmental elements.

Seasonal Jobs

Setting out on an excursion to New Zealand's South Island in 2024 offers a visual banquet of normal miracles as well as the chance to support your movements through occasional positions. Whether you're an explorer, a computerized wanderer, or somebody searching for an interesting work-travel insight, the South Island's occasional work market can be a rewarding road. In this complete aid, we'll investigate how to bring in cash while partaking in the stunning scenes and lively culture of New Zealand's South Island.

Understanding the Occasional Work Scene:

Agribusiness and Cultivation: The South Island is known for its thriving agrarian and plant businesses. Occasional positions frequently incorporate natural product picking, grape plantation work, and homestead work during top gathering seasons.

The travel industry and Cordiality: With a flood in the travel industry during explicit months, organizations in the neighborliness area, like lodgings, eateries, and experience the travel industry organizations, frequently recruit occasional staff.

Working Occasion Visa:

Qualification: Check if you are qualified for a Functioning Occasion Visa. Numerous voyagers select this visa, permitting them to work briefly while investigating the country.

Application Cycle: Exploration the application interaction for the Functioning Occasion Visa and guarantee that you meet every one of the necessities.

Recognizing Occasional Open Positions:

Online Work Stages: Use online work stages and sites that cook explicitly for occasional and brief work. Search for positions in horticulture, friendliness, and the travel industry.

Nearby Work Sheets: Visit neighborhood public venues, lodgings, and notice sheets infamous explorer objections.

Frequently, organizations post occasional open positions in these areas.

Natural product Picking and Homestead Work:

Research Gather Seasons: Various leafy foods have unmistakable collecting seasons. Plan your movements around these seasons to augment open positions.

Lodging and Hiker Associations: Numerous inns and explorer facilities have associations with nearby homesteads. Ask at these spots for potential work leads.

Grape Plantation and Winery Occupations:

Reap Groups: Wineries frequently employ extra staff during grape-collect seasons. Positions might incorporate grape picking, basement work, and general grape plantation upkeep.

Wine Visits and Cordiality: Assuming you have neighborliness abilities, consider working in the tasting rooms of wineries or helping with wine visits.

The Travel Industry and Accommodation Jobs:

Front-of-House Positions: Investigate potential open doors in bistros, cafés, and lodgings for jobs, for example, server team, baristas, or receptionists.

Experience The travel industry: In vacationer areas of interest, experience the travel industry organizations might employ occasional staff for exercises like directing, kayaking, or climbing.

Independent and Remote Work:

Advanced Traveler Open doors: Influence your abilities for remote work. Stages like independent sites, content creation, and internet coaching can turn out a consistent revenue while you travel.

Cooperating Spaces: A few towns in the South Island have collaborating spaces, offering a helpful climate for remote work.

Systems Administration and Building Associations:

Nearby Occasions and Get-togethers: Go to neighborhood occasions, local meetings, and meetups to connect with the two local people and individual explorers. Systems administration can open ways to stow away open positions.

Use Virtual Entertainment: Join online networks and gatherings connected with work and travel in New Zealand. These stages frequently share work leads and tips from experienced voyagers.

Work Trade Projects

Setting out on an excursion to New Zealand's South Island in 2024 doesn't need to be a channel on your funds. Participating in work trade programs offers an amazing open door to drench yourself in the neighborhood culture, meet new individuals, and offset travel costs. Here is an exhaustive aide on the most proficient method to bring in cash through work trade programs while investigating the stunning scenes of the South Island.

Research and Choosing Projects:

Begin by exploring legitimate work trade programs accessible in New Zealand. Sites like Workaway, HelpX, and WWOOF (Overall Open Doors on Natural Homesteads) associate voyagers with needing help with trade for food and lodging.

Assess the kinds of work offered, the terms of the responsibility, and the advantages given by each program before settling on a choice.

Make a Great Profile:

Create a convincing profile exhibiting your abilities, interests, and the sort of work you're chasing. Incorporate pertinent experience, your energy for social trade, and particular abilities that may be important to have.

Recognize Your Inclinations:

Characterize your inclinations concerning the sort of work, area, and length of your visit. Whether you're keen on ranch work, accommodation, or eco-projects, adjust your inclinations to the accessible open doors.

Impart Successfully:

When you track down a likely host, impart successfully. Be clear about your assumptions, ask about the errands in question, and examine the details of the trade. A straightforward and open exchange guarantees a positive encounter for the two players.

Embrace Assorted Work Encounters:

The South Island offers a horde of work trade valuable open doors. From aiding on natural ranches in Marlborough to aiding eco-the travel industry adventures in Fiordland, embrace assorted encounters that line up with your inclinations and abilities.

Figure out Social Assumptions:

Find out about New Zealand's social standards and behavior. Understanding the neighborhood customs and assumptions won't just upgrade your general insight yet in addition assist you with coordinating flawlessly into the local area.

Balance Work and Investigation:

While taking part in work trade, find some kind of harmony between satisfying your obligations and investigating the South Island. Many hosts figure out the craving for investigation and may offer adaptability in planning to permit you to find the locale's normal miracles.

Organization and Fabricate Associations:

Work trade programs are not just about the work; they are tied in with building associations. Network with individual explorers, hosts, and local people. These associations can open up new doors, both expertly and by and by.

Influence Abilities for Extra Pay:

Assuming you have particular abilities, think about offering them for extra pay. Whether it's showing a language, photography, or visual depiction, your abilities can be important to the two hosts and the neighborhood local area.

Remain Consistent with Visa Guidelines:

Guarantee that you are agreeable with New Zealand's visa guidelines for work trade members. A few projects might give direction on visas, however, it's critical to freely check the prerequisites to stay away from lawful complexities.

Establishing a Travel Blog or Vlog

Leaving on an excursion to New Zealand's South Island in 2024 gives you a valuable chance to experience as well as an opportunity to share your encounters and bring in cash through a sightseeing blog or video blog. Laying out an effective travel stage requires vital preparation, imagination, and commitment. In this complete aid, we'll dig into the moves toward assisting you with adapting your touring blog or video blog while investigating the enrapturing scenes of New Zealand's South Island.

Examination and Arranging:

Recognize Your Specialty:

Characterize the focal point of your sightseeing blog or video blog. Whether it's experience travel, extravagant encounters, or social investigation, choosing a specialty will assist you with focusing on a particular crowd.

Understand what Your Listeners might be thinking:

Comprehend your main interest group's inclinations, interests, and socioeconomics. Tailor your substance to impact them, making your blog or video blog more interesting to possible patrons and promoters.

Make Convincing Substance:

Great Visuals:

Put resources into a decent camera and altering devices to guarantee your visuals are enamoring. Excellent photographs and well-altered recordings will make your substance hang out in a jam-packed web-based space.

Drawing in Narrating:

Make convincing stories that transport your crowd to the stunning scenes of the South Island. Share individual encounters, stories, and social bits of knowledge to make an association with your watchers or perusers.

Construct an Expert Brand:

Make a Remarkable Brand Personality:

Plan an outwardly engaging and durable brand personality. This incorporates a particular logo, a variety range, and a noteworthy slogan that mirrors the quintessence of your touring blog or video blog.

Responsive Site or Channel:

Fabricate an easy-to-use site or channel that is portable and responsive. Guarantee simple route and streamline for web indexes to increment permeability.

Connect with Your Crowd:

Online Entertainment Presence:

Influence online entertainment stages to advance your substance and draw in your crowd. Construct a local area around your movement encounters by answering remarks, sharing in the background content, and running intuitive surveys.

Email Promoting:

Make a mailing rundown to keep your crowd refreshed on your most recent undertakings. Use pamphlets to share restrictive substances, travel tips, and limited-time offers.

Adaptation Systems:

Subsidiary Showcasing:

Collaborate with movement-related organizations and procure a commission for every deal produced through your interesting offshoot connect. Advance items or administrations that line up with your image and resound with your crowd.

Supported Content:

Team up with brands and the travel industry sheets for supported content. Exhibit their items, facilities, or encounters in your touring blog or video blog, and haggle fair pay for your administrations.

Promotion Income:

Adapt your site or YouTube channel with promotions. Join promotion networks like Google AdSense to show designated advertisements, producing income-given snaps or impressions.

Item Deals:

Make and sell your product, for example, marked travel gear, digital books, or photography prints. This adds an extra income stream while advancing your image.

Network and Work together:

Interface with Individual Travel Bloggers/Vloggers:

Assemble connections inside the movement's local area by systems administration with different bloggers and vloggers. Team up on projects, share experiences, and cross-elevate each other to extend your compass.

Go to Travel Meetings:

Partake in movement gatherings and systems administration occasions to associate with industry experts, possible supporters, and individual substance makers. These occasions give significant open doors to joint effort and learning.

Improve for Search engine optimization:
Catchphrase Exploration:
Direct careful catchphrase examination to comprehend what terms your crowd is looking for. Upgrade your substance, including blog entries and video portrayals, with pertinent catchphrases to further develop web search tool rankings.

Neighborhood Web Optimization for Area-Based Content:
Considering that you're investigating New Zealand's South Island, streamline your substance for neighborhood Search engine optimization. Use area explicit catchphrases to draw in a crowd of people keen on South Island travel.

Remain Agreeable and Straightforward:
Uncover Coordinated efforts:

Guarantee straightforwardness by plainly uncovering any supported substance or subsidiary connections. Building trust with your crowd is essential for the drawn-out progress of your sightseeing blog or video blog.

Remain Agreeable with Guidelines:
Get to know guidelines concerning supported content, subsidiary advertising, and online advancements. Consistency guarantees you stay away from lawful issues and keep a positive standing.

Assess and Adjust:
Dissect Execution Measurements:
Consistently screen examination to evaluate the presentation of your sightseeing blog or video blog. Track measurements like crowd socioeconomics, commitment, and transformation rates to refine your methodologies.

Adjust to Patterns:

Remain informed about industry drifts and adjust your substance and systems as needed. Embrace arising stages, advancements, and content arrangements to keep your sightseeing blog or video blog important.

Capitalizing on Local Expertise

New Zealand's South Island is a shocking objective that draws in voyagers from around the world. While investigating its stunning scenes and dynamic culture, you can likewise gain neighborhood mastery to enhance your movement reserves. This guide will furnish you with complete bits of knowledge about different ways of bringing in cash while submerging yourself in the special encounters that New Zealand's South Island brings to the table.

Photography and Videography:

Benefit from the pleasant scenes of the South Island by offering your photography or videography abilities. Arrange your work and advance your administrations online through stages like Instagram, Facebook, or committed travel sites. Vacationers frequently look for proficient picture takers to catch their important minutes against the setting of New Zealand's staggering landscape.

Neighborhood Local Escort Administrations:
Influence your insight into the nearby culture, history, and unlikely treasures to turn into an independent local escort. Offer customized visits to individual explorers, displaying the interesting attractions that the South Island brings to the table. Use virtual entertainment and travel discussions to publicize your administrations and fabricate an organization of possible clients.

Culinary Encounters:

If you have an enthusiasm for cooking, consider facilitating culinary encounters for vacationers. Offer cooking classes including conventional New Zealand dishes or put together food-tasting occasions. Utilize neighborhood fixings and team up with ranchers or markets to improve the realness of your culinary endeavors.

Experience Sports Guidance:

New Zealand is famous for its experienced sports scene. On the off chance that you have aptitude in exercises like skiing, snowboarding, or climbing, offer your administration as a teacher. Publicize your abilities in nearby experience sports centers or team up with visit administrators to give novel and exciting encounters to sightseers.

Expressions and Artworks Studios:

Tap into your imaginative side by facilitating expressions and specialties studios. This could incorporate customary Maori specialties, painting, or earthenware. Set up studios in famous traveler regions or team up with nearby displays to exhibit and sell your manifestations.

Language Mentoring:

Assuming you are familiar with various dialects, consider offering language mentoring administrations. Sightseers frequently look for valuable chances to learn nearby expressions and articulations. Publicize your administrations on the web or team up with language schools to give customized examples.

Counseling for Reasonable The travel industry:

Influence your enthusiasm for maintainability by offering counseling administrations to nearby organizations and visit administrators. Give experiences on the best way to make their activities all the more harmless to the ecosystem and socially mindful. Supportable the travel industry is building up some forward movement, and your skill could be sought after.

Advanced Migrant Administrations:

Assuming you have abilities in web improvement, visual communication, or advanced advertising, offer your administrations to nearby organizations needing a web-based presence. Numerous organizations in the South Island might profit from updating their computerized stages to draw in a worldwide crowd.

Utilizing Transportation Services

Going to New Zealand's South Island in 2024 offers a stunning experience as well as any open doors to enhance your pay by decisively using transportation administrations. From the clamoring urban communities to the beautiful open country, the South Island gives material to innovative people to transform their excursion into a rewarding encounter. Here is a thorough aide on the most proficient method to bring in cash while investigating the excellence of New Zealand's South Island through transportation administrations.

Ridesharing and Carpooling:

Stage Usage: Influence ridesharing stages, for example, Uber or nearby administrations to offer rides to individual explorers or local people. Moreover, consider making a carpooling network through online entertainment stages to share transportation costs with different travelers investigating comparable courses.

Nearby Bits of knowledge: Furnish your travelers with experiences into the neighborhood culture, unexpected, yet invaluable treasures, and less popular attractions, offering customized and instructive travel insight.

Bike Rental and Directed Visits:

Lease and Lead Visits: Assuming you're enthusiastic about cycling, think about leasing bikes and offering directed visits through picturesque paths or metropolitan scenes. Give a vivid encounter by sharing your insight into the environmental elements, making it both sporting and instructive.

Modified Bundles: Offer customized bundles, including bicycle rentals, directed visits, and maybe even outing courses of action, taking care of the different inclinations of your clients.

Camper Van Facilitating:

Stage Cooperation: On the off chance that you own a camper van, benefit from the rising pattern of camper van rentals. List your vehicle on stages like Airbnb or committed camper van rental locales to furnish voyagers with a special convenience experience.

Neighborhood Encounters: Upgrade your contribution by including nearby travel tips, suggested campgrounds, and a manual for buried spots, making a sweeping travel bundle.

Air terminal Transport Administrations:

Key Courses: Offer air terminal transport administrations to and from significant air terminals, associating travelers with well-known objections. Center around essential courses to draw in approaching and active explorers, guaranteeing a consistent progression of clients.

Solace and Comfort: Underscore solace and accommodation, giving dependable help to upgrade the general travel insight for your clients.

Comprehensive bundles with Neighborhood Organizations:

Team up with Facilities: Join forces with nearby facilities to offer complete bundles that incorporate transportation administrations. Make packaged bundles that captivate voyagers with a consistent and practical experience.

Cooperative Showcasing: Team up with neighborhood organizations, for example, eateries, experience visit administrators, or social attractions to cross-advance administrations and increment permeability.

Photography and Transportation Bundles:
Photography Administrations: Consolidate transportation administrations with photography bundles, taking care of voyagers hoping to catch their South Island experience. Offer picturesque stops and customized photoshoots, making enduring recollections for your clients.

Web-based Entertainment Promoting: Use online entertainment stages to feature your photography abilities and draw in clients searching for a remarkable travel and photography bundle.

Neighborhood Conveyance Administrations:

Neighborhood Items: Offer a nearby conveyance administration for organizations or people selling handcrafted makes, neighborhood items, or produce. This can incorporate shipping merchandise from provincial regions to metropolitan business sectors or the other way around.

Earth Cognizant: Underline eco-accommodating transportation works, speaking to clients who focus on manageable and neighborhood drives.

Money-Saving Tips and Resources

Leaving on an excursion to New Zealand's South Island in 2024 is a blessing from heaven, and with smart preparation, it very well may be a reasonable and enhancing experience. From investigating the sensational scenes to enjoying the nearby food, here's a thorough aide on useful ways to save cash and assets to capitalize on your Kiwi experience without burning through every last dollar.

Convenience: Embrace Assortment for Spending plan Agreeable Stays

a. Inns and Spending plan Inns: Reasonable Solace

Settle on spending plan amicable convenience choices like lodgings and inns. Stages like Hostelworld and Booking.com offer a scope of decisions, permitting you to track down reasonable yet agreeable spots to remain across the South Island.

b. Setting up camp: Associate with Nature

Exploit New Zealand's dazzling landscape by setting up camp in assigned camping areas or opportunity setting up camp regions. Put resources into a quality tent, and use applications like CamperMate to find free or minimal expense setting up camp spots, guaranteeing an essential encounter under the Southern Side of the equator's brilliant skies.

Transportation: Explore Productively and Financially

a. Public Transportation: Investigate effortlessly

Use New Zealand's very much associated public transportation framework. Transports and trains offer financially savvy choices for getting around, giving panoramic detours that permit you to partake in the scenes while saving money on fuel and rental expenses.

b. Vehicle Rentals: Analyze and Book Ahead of time

If you favor the adaptability of a vehicle, look at rental costs on stages like Rentalcars.com and book ahead of time to get the best rates. Carpooling applications like ShareRing can likewise associate you with individual explorers to share costs.

Food and Eating: Enjoy Nearby Flavors on a Careful spending plan

a. Neighborhood Markets: New and Reasonable Produce

Investigate nearby business sectors to buy new produce, tidbits, and dinners at sensible costs. Ranchers' business sectors are a culinary pleasure as well as a magnificent method for supporting neighborhood organizations while remaining inside the spending plan.

b. Cook Your Feasts: Inn Kitchens and Open air fire Cooking

Save money on eating costs by setting up your feasts. Pick facilities with collective kitchens, and exploit New Zealand's various public grill offices for a genuine Kiwi culinary experience.

Exercises and Attractions: Embrace Free and Limited Undertakings

a. Free Exercises: Nature's Abundance

A significant number of New Zealand's attractions are regular ponders that accompany no section expense. Investigate public parks, climbing trails, and seashores to partake in the stunning magnificence of the South Island without spending a dime.

b. Rebate Passes: Investigate Financially

Put resources into fascination passes and rebate cards like the Kiwi Experience or the DOC (Division of Protection) pass. These propositions admittance to various attractions and exercises at a scaled-down cost, permitting you to capitalize on your spending plan.

Correspondence and Availability: Remain Associated without Overspending

a. Neighborhood SIM Cards: Reasonable Information and Calls

Buy a neighborhood SIM card for your telephone to profit from reasonable information plans and calling rates. This guarantees that you stay associated with companions, family, and individual explorers without causing heavy worldwide meandering charges.

b. Free Wi-Fi: Use Public Areas of interest

Influence free Wi-Fi accessible in bistros, libraries, and public spaces. This will assist you with remaining associated without the requirement for exorbitant versatile information utilization.

Legal and Practical Considerations

Leaving on an excursion to New Zealand's South Island in 2024 can be a little glimpse of heaven, particularly on the off chance that you intend to bring in cash while partaking in the staggering scenes. In any case, before you dig into the domain of remote work, occasional positions, or enterprising undertakings, it's pivotal to be very informed about lawful and functional contemplations to guarantee a smooth and consistent experience. In this aid, we'll investigate the vital stages and precautionary measures to take while bringing in cash in New Zealand and appreciating the miracles of the South Island.

Visa and Work Approval:

Working Occasion Visa: If you are arranging a long-term visit and wish to work, consider applying for a Functioning Occasion Visa. Guarantee you meet the qualification measures and go through the application cycle well ahead of time.

Other Visa Choices: Research other visa choices if you intend to take part in more specific work, for example, a work visa or explicit licenses connected with your calling.

Charge Commitments:

IRD Number: Acquire an Inland Income Division (IRD) number upon appearance. This novel identifier is vital for charge purposes and lawful work.

Charge Residency: Comprehend the idea of expense residency in New Zealand to decide your duty commitments in light of your visit term and pay.

Grasping Nearby Work Regulations:

Business Agreements: If you secure some work, find out more about New Zealand's business regulations. Work agreements ought to frame your privileges, obligations, and states of business.

The lowest pay permitted by law: Know about the lowest pay permitted by law prerequisites to guarantee fair remuneration for your work.

Remote Work and Computerized Nomadism:

Web Availability: Guarantee you have a dependable web network, particularly assuming you intend to remotely work. Numerous towns in the South Island offer a great network, yet checking in advance is savvy.

Time Region Contemplations: If working with clients or a group in an alternate time region, plan your functioning hours as needed to keep up with successful correspondence.

Occasional Positions and Rural Work:

Wellbeing and Security Guidelines: Occupations in agribusiness might include actual work. Know about well-being and security guidelines and comply with working environment rules to forestall wounds.

Convenience and Transportation: For occasional positions, consider the accessibility of reasonable convenience and dependable transportation to and from work areas.

Pioneering Pursuits:

Business Enrollment: If you intend to begin a private company or proposition administration, research the legitimate necessities for business enlistment and permitting.

Nearby Guidelines: Conform to neighborhood guidelines and get any vital licenses or endorsements for your business exercises.

Protection Inclusion:

Health care coverage: Guarantee you have far-reaching health care coverage inclusion as long as necessary. New Zealand's public medical care framework may not cover all clinical costs for guests.

Travel Protection: Think about movement protection that covers unforeseen occasions, undoings, and loss of possessions.

Social Responsiveness and Joining:

Regard Neighborhood Culture: Find out more about New Zealand's social standards and values to incorporate consistently into the nearby local area.

Organization and Construct Connections: Interface with local people and individual voyagers to fabricate a strong organization. Systems administration can give significant experience in open positions and commonsense guidance.

CHAPTER SEVEN

Conclusion

As we bid goodbye to the pages of "Finding Heaven: A Far-reaching Manual for Special New Zealand's South Island - 2024 Travel Edition," we believe that this excursion through the core of Aotearoa has been as improving for you as it has been for us. Your investigation of the South Island isn't just a touristic try; it's a journey into the spirit blending magnificence, social extravagance, and untamed soul of this wonderful district.

Over this aid, we've explored the great Southern Alps, felt overwhelmed before the mirror-like lakes, and wondered about the fjords carved into the scene like nature's own magnum opuses. We've meandered through lively urban areas, retaining the beat of advancement, and dove into the immortal customs of the Maori public, whose legacy is joined with the actual texture of the land.

Our point was to give data as well as to move a significant association between you and the miracles of the South Island. We trust you've felt the thrill of scaling mountain tops, the quietness of sapphire-blue lakes, and the glow of Kiwi friendliness. Each proposal, everything about it, is cautiously organized to guarantee your experience rises above the normal and turns into an embroidery of remarkable minutes.

In this release, we have additionally stressed the significance of capable travel and manageable practices. The future of investigating heavens like the South Island lies in our grasp, and by taking on eco-accommodating propensities and supporting nearby drives, we can guarantee that these perfect scenes persevere for a long time into the future. Travel, all things considered, isn't just about seeing new spots yet in addition about safeguarding them for what's in store.

As you turn the last page, we urge you to convey the quintessence of the South Island with you. Allow its scenes to rouse your fantasies, its social embroidered artwork tone your perspective, and its soul of experience push you toward new skylines. The recollections you've gathered here are not simple keepsakes but rather getting through engraves on the material of your life.

That's what our genuine expectation is "Finding Heaven" fills in as your devoted friend, directing you through the strange domains of the South Island and leaving you with a feeling of satisfaction and a desire for new experiences that waits long after you've gotten back. May the reverberations of your strides in this perfect wild keep on resounding, coaxing you back to the charm that is Exceptional New Zealand's South Island. Once more, until we meet, cheerful voyages, and may your undertakings be essentially as vast as the scenes you've come to esteem.

Printed in Great Britain
by Amazon

57719929R00116